my revisi⏻n notes

Edexcel AS/A-level History

SOUTH AFRICA, 1948–94

FROM APARTHEID STATE TO 'RAINBOW NATION'

Peter Clements

Series editor
Peter Callaghan

D1512749

ANDOVER COLLEGE

HODDER
EDUCATION
AN HACHETTE UK COMPANY

Acknowledgements

The Publishers would like to thank the following for permission to reproduce copyright material.

p.19 *S1* Excerpts from 'Spectre of Belsen and Buchenwald: Life Under Apartheid' by Nelson Mandela, October 1955. http://www.anc.org.za/content/spectre-belsen-and-buchenwald-life-under-apartheid-nelson-mandela; **p.21** *S1* Excerpts from ANC Programme of Action dated 17 December 1949. http://www.anc.org.za/content/38th-national-conference-programme-action-statement-policy-adopted; **p.24** *S2* & **p.73** *S2* Excerpts from *Nelson Mandela: Long Walk to Freedom*, by Nelson Mandela. Used with permission of the publisher Little, Brown Book Group; **p.27** *S1* Excerpts from *Africa South in Exile*, Vol 4 No 4 July–September 1960; **p.47** *S1* Excerpts from the editorial of 'The Will of an Entire People – Forged Under Fire', published in the magazine *Sechaba* (Vol 11), published in 1977; **p.51** *S2* & **p.60** *S2* Contains public sector information licensed under the Open Government Licence v3.0; **p.57** *S2* 'Human Rights in Namibia', a paper given by Nora Chase, given at the Black Sash Annual Conference in March 1988. http://www.sahistory.org.za/archive/human-rights-in-namibia-10-years-after-security-council-resolution-435-paper-presented-at-the-black-sash-national-conference-1988. Also available in *SASH*, June 1988, p.19.

Every effort has been made to trace all copyright holders, but if any have been inadvertently overlooked, the Publishers will be pleased to make the necessary arrangements at the first opportunity.

Although every effort has been made to ensure that website addresses are correct at time of going to press, Hodder Education cannot be held responsible for the content of any website mentioned in this book. It is sometimes possible to find a relocated web page by typing in the address of the home page for a website in the URL window of your browser.

Hachette UK's policy is to use papers that are natural, renewable and recyclable products and made from wood grown in sustainable forests. The logging and manufacturing processes are expected to conform to the environmental regulations of the country of origin.

Orders: please contact Bookpoint Ltd, 130 Milton Park, Abingdon, Oxon OX14 4SE. Telephone: +44 (0)1235 827720. Fax: +44 (0)1235 400401. Email education@bookpoint.co.uk Lines are open from 9 a.m. to 5 p.m., Monday to Saturday, with a 24-hour message answering service. You can also order through our website: www.hoddereducation.co.uk

ISBN: 978 1 5104 1812 7

© Peter Clements 2018

First published in 2018 by
Hodder Education,
An Hachette UK Company
Carmelite House
50 Victoria Embankment
London EC4Y 0DZ

www.hoddereducation.co.uk

Impression number   10 9 8 7 6 5 4 3 2

Year   2022 2021 2020 2019 2018

Cover photo © mozZz – stock.adobe.com
Illustrations by Integra
Typeset by Integra Software Services, Pvt, Ltd, Pondicherrry, India
Printed in Spain

A catalogue record for this title is available from the British Library.

My Revision Planner

REVISED

Introduction

About Paper 2

Paper 2 Option 2F.2: South Africa 1948–94 is a depth study. Therefore it requires a detailed knowledge of the period that you are studying. Paper 2 tests you against two Assessment Objectives: AO1 and AO2.

AO1 tests your ability to:
- organise and communicate your own knowledge
- analyse and evaluate key features of the past
- make supported judgements
- deal with concepts of cause, consequence, change, continuity, similarity, difference and significance.

On Paper 2, AO1 tasks require you to write an essay from your own knowledge.

AO2 tests your ability to:
- analyse and evaluate source material from the past
- explore the value of source material by considering its historical context.

On Paper 2, the AO2 task requires you to write an essay which analyses two sources which come from the period you have studied. At A-level, Paper 2 is worth 20 per cent of your qualification. At AS level, Paper 2 is worth 40 per cent of your qualification. Significantly, your AS grade does not count towards your overall A-level grade. Therefore, you will have to take this paper at A-level in order to get the A-level qualification.

Structure

At AS and A-level, Paper 2 is structured around four key topics which cover the period 1948 to 1994. The AS and A-level exams are divided into two sections. Section A tests your source analysis skills, whereas Section B tests your ability to write an essay from own knowledge. Both sections focus on the four key topics. The question may deal with aspects of one of the topics, or may be set on issues that require knowledge of several or all of the topics.

Aspect of the course	AO	Exam
Key Topic 1: The response to apartheid, c.1948–59		
Key Topic 2: Radicalisation of resistance and the consolidation of National Party power, 1960–68	AO1 & AO2	Section A and Section B
Key Topic 3: Redefining resistance and challenges to National Party power, 1968–83		
Key Topic 4: The end of apartheid and the creation of the 'rainbow nation', 1984–94		

The exam

At AS and A-level, the Paper 2 exam lasts for 1 hour and 30 minutes. It is divided into two sections, both of which test the depth of your historical knowledge.

How to use this book

This book has been designed to help you to develop the knowledge and skills necessary to succeed in this exam. The book is divided into four sections – one for each of the key topics. Each section is made up of a series of topics organised into double-page spreads. On the left-hand page, you will find a summary of the key content you need to learn. Words in bold in the key content are defined in the glossary. On the right-hand page, you will find exam-focused activities.

Together, these two strands of the book will take you through the knowledge and skills essential for exam success.

There are three levels of exam-focused activities.
- **Band 1** activities are designed to develop the foundation skills needed to pass the exam.
- **Band 2** activities are designed to build on the skills developed in Band 1 activities and to help you to achieve a C grade.
- **Band 3** activities are designed to enable you to access the highest grades.

Some of the activities have answers or suggested answers on page 87. These have the following symbol to indicate this:

Each section ends with an exam-style question and model high-level answer with examiner's commentary. This should give you guidance on what is required to achieve the top grades.

Mark schemes

For some of the activities in the book it will be useful to refer to the mark scheme. Paper 1 requires two mark schemes, one for the AO2 assessments in Section A and another for Section B's AO2 assessment. Mark schemes can be found at the back of the book.

1 The response to apartheid, c.1948–59

Race, segregation and discrimination

In 1948, South Africa's population consisted of four racial groups:

- Black Africans, the largest group descended from the indigenous inhabitants.
- Coloureds, or descendants of mixed marriages, who lived mainly in Cape Province. From around 1950 to 1990, under apartheid, 'coloured' was legally defined as 'a person of mixed European ('white') and African ('black') or Asian ancestry'. That is why we use this term in this book. It is, of course, derogatory today to use this word.
- Asians, mainly of Indian origin, who had grown into a merchant and administrative class. They lived mainly in the province of Natal.
- Whites, comprised of Afrikaans and English speakers, with tensions between them. Until 1948 Afrikaners felt the English speakers dominated both economically and politically.

South Africa's population, 1946

Ethnic group	Population
Black Africans (many different groups)	7,830,559
White	2,372,044
Coloured	928,062
Indian	285,260

The different races of South Africa were strictly segregated. With only a few exceptions, whites were the only racial group who could vote. (The right of coloured people to vote was protected by the 1910 constitution, but they were eventually disenfranchised in 1956.) Black Africans in particular were treated as cheap labour, unable to compete with whites for whom the best jobs were reserved.

Pass laws

All black male migrant workers had to carry passes, a type of internal passport system. Each province issued its own passes so there was no centralised system until 1952 (see page 14).

Three laws affecting Africans

1913	Native Land Act	Land ownership limited to tribal reserves: 7% of total land in South Africa
1923	Urban Areas Act	Must live in townships in white areas
1936	Native Trusts and Lands Act	Tribal reserves could be extended to 13.6% of total land area of South Africa

Black Africans were overwhelmingly the largest racial grouping but all political and economic power was effectively monopolised by the whites.

Urbanisation and industrialisation

Although mainly rural, white South Africa grew more urban and industrial as the twentieth century developed. This was as a result in particular of the growth of the mining industry – gold, diamonds and precious metals for example, which South Africa relied on for much of its wealth. Large quantities of diamonds had been discovered in the Kimberley region of the Orange Free State in 1867 and gold in the Transvaal in 1887, which led to a huge demand for African transient (migrant) workers. Elsewhere the South African economy remained mainly agricultural.

African urbanisation

There was always a tension between the desire to prevent Africans moving into areas reserved for whites and the need for cheap labour. In theory Africans worked on temporary contracts and had to return to the tribal areas allocated to them when these contracts ended; in practice it is estimated that in the period 1919 to 1939 every African male went to work for whites at some point during his life. By 1946, 23 per cent of Africans were living in urban areas – as opposed to 75 per cent of whites, 61 per cent of coloureds and 71 per cent of Indians.

Township life

Transient workers lived either in single sex barracks or in townships. These were special settlements on the edge of urban areas, with basic homes for urban African workers. These were often overcrowded, insanitary and squalid and were to continue until the end of the apartheid period. 'Apartheid' is the word used to refer to the strict separation of different racial groups in South Africa at this time. In Afrikaans, the word means 'separate' or 'apartness'.

Spot the mistake   a

Below are a sample exam question and a paragraph written in answer to this question. Why does this paragraph not get into Level 4? Once you have identified the mistake, rewrite the paragraph so that it displays the qualities of Level 4. The mark scheme on page 86 will help you.

How far do you agree that black Africans faced discrimination before 1948?

> In 1948, South Africa was made up of four racial groups: black Africans, the largest group descended from the people who originally lived there; coloureds, or descendants of mixed marriages, who lived mainly in Cape Province; Asians, mainly of Indian origin, had grown into a merchant and administrative class; and whites comprised of Afrikaans and English speakers. Most whites had racist views of Africans being lazy, untrustworthy and, potentially, dangerous. They feared being swamped by blacks if they were allowed to live in white areas. However, they did need them for cheap labour. Indeed all non-white groups faced discrimination. Only whites could vote and they held most of the wealth.

 Complete the paragraph

Below are a sample exam question and a paragraph written in answer to this question. The paragraph contains a point and specific examples, but lacks a concluding analytical link back to the question. Complete the paragraph, adding this link in the space provided.

'Black South Africans were urbanised to a considerable degree before 1948.' To what extent do you agree with this statement?

> Technically blacks had no right of permanent residence on white areas. There were two key pieces of legislation which forced the races to live apart: the 1913 Natives Land Act, which restricted black land ownership to the 7 per cent reserved for them in their tribal homelands, and the 1936 Native Trust and Land Act, which extended this to 13 per cent. In addition in 1923 the Native Areas Act limited their rights to live in the white areas of South Africa to townships on the outskirts of cities. In theory Africans worked on temporary contracts and had to return to the tribal areas allocated to them when these contracts ended. The vast majority of blacks lived in their mainly rural tribal homelands and rarely came into contact with other groups. However, there was always a need for cheap black African labour and they increasingly moved to find work in the cities. It is estimated that in the period 1919 to 1939 every African male went to work for whites at some point during his life. As a result the percentage of black Africans as the population of white cities rose from 16 per cent in 1921, to 21 per cent by 1936, to 23 per cent by 1946. Overall...
>
> _____
>
> _____

Afrikaner culture and politics

Afrikaner culture

Afrikaners were descended from white settlers called Boers who came largely from Holland and Germany in the late eighteenth and early nineteenth century; their language, Afrikaans, is derived from German and Dutch.

As time went on, Afrikaners developed their own culture, separate from British or European. They were conscious that, unlike the British, they had no 'mother country' as such, and nowhere to go to should their life in South Africa fail; some commentators called them the white tribe of Africa.

Afrikaner characteristics

As a people Afrikaners were characterised by:

● hard work, mainly farming land that was often naturally infertile

● a stern puritanical Christianity: a belief in the literal truth of the Bible, and a rejection of what were considered 'pleasures of the flesh', such as alcohol

● extreme racism: believing that non-white people were inferior; some even believed non-white people had been cursed by God

● a 'laager mentality', exemplified by their determination to proceed with apartheid and white supremacy despite opposition internally and internationally: indeed the greater the opposition the greater the determination.

History

The relationship between them and the British was always uneasy. When the British abolished slavery within the British Empire in 1833, many of the Boer settlers who kept slaves then moved into the vast hinterland away from British rule. This was called the Great Trek and became a sacred event for future generations of Afrikaners. On the eve of the Battle of Blood River against the Zulus in 1838, they were alleged to have a Covenant with God asking for victory. This subsequently became the basis of their belief that God had granted them the land of South Africa.

Afrikaner history was based on the myth that they marched into an empty land – and black African homelands were comprised of the 7 (later 13) per cent of the land, which was all they allegedly lived on in the 1830s.

White justification for segregation

Most whites had racist views as Africans being lazy, untrustworthy and, potentially, dangerous. These views were largely based on two factors:

● Ignorance and fears for their own safety if Africans were given political or economic rights.

● A belief that segregation from whites was in the Africans' best interests – that they were most happy and contented living separately from white people and in a simple pastoral environment.

Afrikaner politics (before the Second World War)

All the political parties vying for power were comprised almost exclusively of whites. Afrikaners often felt excluded from power: the most successful parties were dominated by English speakers and legislated, they believed, in the interests of these citizens – although they did pass segregationalist legislation.

However, during the interwar years Afrikaners developed their own identity and institutions: this included the Broederbund, a hugely influential movement set up in 1918 and dedicated to promoting their interests: during the apartheid era from 1948 to 1994 every South African leader was a member. After various struggles and mergers, the main Afrikaner party emerged as the National Party, which promoted Afrikaner identity and values and was intent on imposing a system of apartheid, white supremacy and reducing ties with Britain.

The influence of Britain

South Africa had been a dominion within the British Empire since 1910. English-speaking parties dominated the South African government during the interwar years, although they were just as racist and segregationalist as the National Party.

However, Afrikaners resented British influence:

● They had been defeated in the Boer War of 1899 to 1902 to expel the British and resented the settlement which saw South Africa created as a British dominion.

● They had resented South Africa supporting Britain in the First World War: many had strong ties to Germany.

● They resented English speakers' dominance in the economy.

Support or challenge?

Below is a sample exam question which asks how far you agree with a specific statement. Below this is a series of general statements which are relevant to the question. Using your own knowledge and the information on the opposite page, decide whether these statements support or challenge the statement in the question and tick the appropriate box.

How far do you agree that there were fundamental tensions about the development of South Africa between the English and Afrikaner South Africans?

	Support	Challenge
Both English and Afrikaner South Africans believed in white supremacy.		
Afrikaners resented what they felt was English domination of the economy and politics.		
The Broederbund promoted Afrikaner interests.		
The National Party wished to reduce ties with Britain.		
Segregationalist policies pre-dated the National Party electoral victory in 1948.		

Spot the inference (AO2) **a**

High-level answers avoid excessive summarising or paraphrasing the sources. They instead make inferences from the sources, as well as analysing their value in terms of their context. Below are a source and a series of statements. Read the source and decide which of the statements:

- make inferences from the source (I)
- paraphrase the source (P)
- summarise the source (S)
- cannot be justified from the source (X).

		I	P	S	X
1	Afrikaners are becoming more involved in commerce and industry, following the success of English South Africans in these fields.				
2	Although Afrikaners and English-speaking South Africans are growing closer together, there are still fundamental differences between them.				
3	English South Africans remain nostalgic about Britain.				
4	English South Africans and Afrikaners share a common culture.				
5	English South Africans were quicker to embrace industry and commerce than Afrikaners.				

SOURCE

From Roy MacNab, Union of South Africa, an Essay in South and Southern Africa, *published in 1954. The book forms part of a series of guides to different geographical areas.*

It has been in commerce and industry, particularly mining, that English South Africans have contributed most to their country. The great mining houses ... are all the creation of English South Africans, and it is on their skill and ingenuity, their enterprise and vision that modern South Africa has been evolved and their example in this field that the Afrikaner is today so successfully emulating.

As time goes on the differences grow fewer between English and Afrikaans speaking South Africans as they share more and more of each other's lives. There are some who already believe a distinct South African type has been evolved. Nevertheless the English South African, even of the fourth and fifth generation, is still very conscious of his ties with Britain, to which until a decade ago he referred to as home or the old country. The English South African is in a difficult position vis-a-vis his Afrikaans speaking colleague. The Afrikaner broke away completely from his homeland which in most cases was Holland. This was not a necessarily a conscious act, but rather forces of history ensured his isolation from Europe.

Reasons for the National Party victory in 1948

In the 1948 elections, the National Party won 79 seats to the United Party's 71. The new government was committed to an extensive policy of apartheid in which the races were segregated as far as possible. The National Party was to win every further election until the demise of apartheid in 1994.

National Party leaders of government, 1948–94

Name	Years	Reason for leaving
D.F. Malan	1948–54	Retirement
J.G. Strijdom	1954–58	Death from cancer
H. Verwoerd	1958–66	Assassination
J. Vorster	1966–79	Resignation
P.W. Botha	1979–89	Ill-health
F.W. de Klerk	1989–94	Electoral defeat

The National Party won the election for many reasons: the outgoing Prime Minister Jan Smuts was old and tired and his campaign lacked lustre. No new policies were on offer. However, there were fundamental underlying reasons for the victory.

The impact of the Second World War

The outbreak of the Second World War divided the whites. English speakers were more likely to support the Allies while Afrikaners often felt affinity with Nazi Germany. Hendrik Verwoerd, a future prime minister, became the editor of *Die Transvaler*, the newspaper of the National Party. This became notorious during the war not only for its pro-Nazi stance but also for its anti-Semitism.

Economic effects of war

The need for labour meant many of the laws relating to the employment of Africans were relaxed: of the 125,000 extra workers employed in manufacturing during the war years, just 25 per cent were white. Although Africans received far less pay than whites, many Afrikaners feared Africans would take their jobs once the war was over. In particular they feared the ruling United Party, under the guidance of Deputy Prime Minister Jan Hofmeyr, was preparing a more moderate racial policy.

The growth of Afrikaner nationalism

Afrikaners were becoming more assertive and developing the National Party: they were organising at local levels to win support and developing strategies for the achievement of power.

- They did not trust the English-speaking parties.
- In 1938 the **Voortrekker monument**, celebrating the centenary of the Battle of Blood River, was built: it created a real sense of Afrikaner identity.

- Afrikaner finance concerns were developed to help Afrikaners set up their own businesses.
- The **Dutch Reformed Church** provided Afrikaner schools and cultural activities to develop a pride in Afrikaner identity.

Fear of United Party moderation of racial policies

Many whites distrusted the United Party on its racial policies. During the election campaign Smuts suggested the influx of Africans into white areas for employment could continue. Although he emphasised Africans should continue to live in strictly segregated and regulated communities, the National Party focused much of their campaign attacks on this policy.

Afrikaner support for the Nazis

While half the white South African male population of military age – 180,000 men – joined the Allied forces, some Afrikaners actively worked for a Nazi victory, for example by broadcasting and publishing pro-Nazi material. Many joined the openly pro-fascist Greyshirt movement, or supported the Oxwagon Sentinel formed after the Battle of Blood River centenary and modelled on the Nazi Party. It claimed 250,000 members by 1939. Many were interned as potential traitors during the war years.

International pressures for change

The international response to the National Party victory was muted because many European countries such as Britain and France still had empires in which the indigenous populations were subservient. South Africa was surrounded by pliant neighbours such as Rhodesia, part of the British Empire, and Angola and Mozambique, governed by Portugal. South Africa was itself in charge of South West Africa (Namibia), to its north-east.

However, international criticism grew, particularly as anti-colonial movements developed.

United Nations

The first international discussion on apartheid had been initiated by India concerned about the treatment of Indians in South Africa as early as 1946. Thereafter the **UN General Council** condemned apartheid every year from 1952.

However, the USA was very influential within the **United Nations**, especially in its **Security Council**. South Africa avoided pressure to change because it was seen as a reliable ally against the growth of **communism**, and profitable for investment. The situation was to change significantly by the end of the 1950s but, initially at least, the South African government was free to act without international coercion.

Delete as applicable

Below are a sample exam question and a paragraph written in answer to this question. Read the paragraph and decide which of the possible options (in bold) is most appropriate. Delete the least appropriate options and complete the paragraph by justifying your selection.

To what extent was the growth of Afrikaner nationalism the main reason for the success of the National Party in the 1948 elections?

The growth of Afrikaner identity was, to a **large/fair/limited** extent, the main reason for the success of the National Party in the 1948 elections. For example, the Broederbund had been set up to promote Afrikaner interests while political activists organised support at local levels to develop grassroots support. The celebration of the centenary of the Battle of Blood River in 1938 helped forge a real sense of Afrikaner identity. There was widespread distrust of the English-dominated parties which had formed the pre-war government. Indeed the impact of the Second World War had a significant effect because many Afrikaners resented South African involvement: many supported the Nazis. However, one must also consider other factors — the campaign of the United Party lacked effectiveness and its leaders were seen as tired. It seemed weak on racial policies, and many feared it would adopt a more liberal policy, for example making more types of jobs available to black South Africans. Overall, however, the growth of Afrikaner identity was the **major/minor/jointly important** reason for the success of the National Party because . . .

_____

_____

Mind map

Use the information on the opposite page to add detail to the mind map below.

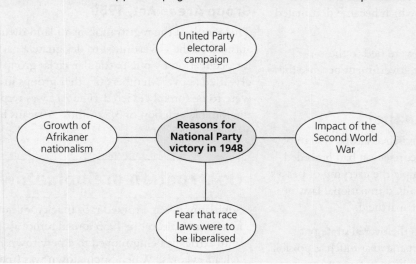

Implementing apartheid: Strengthening the National Party

The years 1948 to 1959 saw the effective implantation of apartheid in all its forms and the development of the National Party as the natural party of government in South Africa.

The new government sought to impose white supremacy through an all-embracing system of apartheid.

Development of National Party government control

The National Party didn't have precise blueprints for the implementation of apartheid. Their main ambition in the early years of their government was to stay in power. However, apartheid was the centre of their platform. They maintained their support and achieved apartheid by various strategies:

- Making the state more dominated by Afrikaners; for example, as English-speaking civil servants retired, they were replaced by Afrikaners.
- All senior National Party politicians and government officials were expected to have close ties with the Broederbund.
- They created new political constituencies, for example in South West Africa (Namibia).
- In 1956 they disenfranchised coloured voters.

Growth in National Party support

The party grew in support: by the elections of 1958 and 1961 it had a majority of over 50 seats which it was able to retain throughout the apartheid period. This was due both to party organisation and control, and the development of a bureaucracy which became dominated by Afrikaners.

Many Afrikaners quite simply were tied to the continuation of National Party government because they relied on it for their livelihoods.

Grand and petty apartheid

The National Party strategy envisaged a total system of apartheid. Many examples of segregation had preceded their electoral victory, for example the carrying of passes. Now, however, it was all formalised in national law. There were two broad types of apartheid.

- **Grand apartheid**: This was the overall strategy of keeping the different races separated as much as possible, for example by ensuring they lived in separate areas.
- **Petty apartheid**: This was the day-to-day restrictions such as separate facilities. Many Africans found this more wearying than grand apartheid.

Apartheid laws

Race relations dominated South Africa's government during the apartheid period. While many Acts were introduced to cover every possible aspect of racial division, the cornerstone was the 1950 Population Registration Act.

Population Registration Act, 1950

This Act designated the racial category of everyone, divided initially into black, white and coloured, with 'Indian' added later. It insisted the different groups be kept strictly separate. Husbands and wives in interracial (mixed) marriages were expected to split up. Everyone was registered according to their racial group and issued with an identity card with their racial group appended. There were tests created and carried out to determine which category a person belonged to.

As Malan asserted, one significant effect of registration according to race was that it put an end to mixed (interracial) marriages and relationships.

Prohibition of Mixed Marriages Act, 1949, and Immorality Act, 1950

In 1949 and 1950 respectively, mixed marriages and sexual relations between members of different racial groups were made illegal. Whites could be imprisoned for disobeying the latter, although their punishment was not usually as severe as for members of other groups, including their sexual partners.

Group Areas Act, 1950

This required the registration of all land ownership and authorised the government to designate a particular area for occupation by one particular racial group as classified above. Members of other groups in this area were to be forcibly evicted. The Act was responsible for the forcible eviction of 3.5 million Africans between 1951 and 1986.

Destruction of Sophiatown

Sophiatown was a mixed race **blackspot** noted for its vibrant culture. In 1953 forced removals began, with Africans being moved to a new township, 'Meadowlands'. When Sophiatown was finally demolished it was replaced by a white suburb named Triomf.

Explain the difference

The following sources give different accounts of the impact of apartheid legislation. List the ways in which the sources differ. Explain the differences between the sources using the provenance of the sources, and the historical context. The provenance appears at the top of the source. Make sure you stay focused on the differences that are relevant to the question.

How far could the historian make use of Sources 1 and 2 together to investigate the impact of apartheid legislation? Explain your answer, using both sources, the information given about them and your own knowledge of the historical context.

SOURCE 1

Extracts from the Population Registration Act 1950.

...'white person' means a person who in appearance obviously is, or who is generally accepted as a white person, but does not include a person who, although in appearance obviously a white person, is generally accepted as a coloured person...

5. (1) Every person whose name is included in the register shall be classified by the Director as a white person, a coloured person or a native, as the case may be, and every coloured person and every native whose name is so included shall be classified by the Director according to the ethnic or other group to which he belongs...

11. (1) Any person who considers himself aggrieved by his classification by the Director in terms of section five, and any person who has any objection to the classification of any other person in terms of the said section, may at any time object in writing to the Director against that classification...

(3) Every objection received by the Director in terms of sub-section (2) shall be referred by him for decision to a board of not less than three persons, including the chairman, constituted for the purpose by the Minister, and presided over by a person, appointed by the Minister, who is or has been a judge of the Supreme Court of South Africa, or a magistrate. Provided that no objection which relates to the classification of a person other than the objector shall be so referred for decision unless the objector has paid the deposit referred to in sub-section (4).

SOURCE 2

Extract from 'Not Even Invited to the Party', an essay written in 1983 by Archbishop Desmond Tutu, from a compilation of his writings, The Rainbow People of God, *published in 1994. Tutu is an influential and well-respected anti-apartheid campaigner.*

Apartheid is upheld by a phalanx of ubiquitous laws, such as the Population Registration Act, which decrees that all South Africans must be classified ethnically and duly registered according to these race categories. Many times, in the same family one child has been classified white whilst another with a slightly darker hue has been classified coloured, with all the horrible consequences for the latter of being shut out from membership of a greatly privileged caste. There have been as a result several child suicides. This is too high a price to pay for racial purity, for it is doubtful whether any end, however desirable, can justify such a means. There are laws such as the Prohibition of Mixed Marriages Act which regard marriages between a white and a person of another race as illegal. Race becomes an impediment to a valid marriage.

Pass laws and education

The system of apartheid enabled the treatment of black Africans (commonly referred to as 'Bantu') as a subservient race, only tolerated as guest workers in white South Africa. On a day-to-day level, this was seen most clearly through pass laws and education.

Pass laws: Native Laws Amendment Act, 1952

This Act was also known as the Abolition of Passes and Co-ordination of Documents Act. It standardised the use of passes by Africans throughout South Africa, by officially abolishing existing passes and replacing them with reference books. It stated specifically that all non-white people, including for the first time women, needed to carry their pass book (see page 6) to enter the white areas.

The Act's purpose was to standardise the use of passes throughout South Africa. The abolition of passes and their replacement with reference books was simply a matter of form. The use of passes in practice became even more rigorously enforced.

Education: Bantu Education Act, 1953

This was largely the brainchild of Minister for Native Affairs, Verwoerd, and the **Eiselen Commission** he appointed in 1949 to investigate African education.

Education before the National Party victory

The vast majority of education for Africans was provided by church-run **mission schools**. In 1945 there were 4360 mission schools and 230 government-run ones.

By 1948, the system was breaking down. With poor funding, often dilapidated buildings and insufficient resources, the schools could no longer maintain their standards. The rise in African populations and urbanisation meant they were vastly overcrowded and regularly had to turn prospective students away. The reality was that less than 33 per cent of African children attended school at all.

The Bantu Education Act, 1953

This Act:

- removed control of African education from the Ministry of Education to the Ministry for Native Affairs
- removed state subsidies from mission schools so most were forced to close

- expanded the government-run system and set a limited vocational-based curriculum.

The work of the Department of Native Affairs grew significantly; for example, the Act gave them management of 26,000 African teachers. In 1958 a separate Department of Bantu Education was created to meet this increased workload.

The Tomlinson Report and Bantustans

The Bantu Authorities Act 1951 reiterated that Africans could only live permanently on their **tribal reserves** or Bantustans. ('Bantustans' was the name given to tribal homelands, where people were supposedly responsible for their own affairs.) These were to be governed by tribal leaders designated by the government. However, these could be deposed if uncooperative (see page 20). Tribal leaders were ostensibly responsible for allocation of land, development programmes and welfare policies.

The Tomlinson Commission in 1956 reported on how the homelands might be developed. Its report reasserted that:

- homelands could never support more than two-thirds of their populations, and advised more land be allocated
- policies of **betterment** be developed to combat problems such as soil erosion; it was estimated that cost of this would be at least £100 million
- the agricultural workforce be reduced; industrial concerns could be developed just outside the borders and towns developed just within, so homeland residents could commute for employment.

The government broadly accepted the report's findings although it had no intention of providing more land, and disliked the recommendations concerning industrial developments because with the use of cheap labour such ventures would undercut white-staffed competitors.

The Bantu Self-Government Act, 1959

This set up eight self-governing homelands in which black Africans were to be citizens. By removing them officially from South African statistics, whites would effectively be the largest racial group in South Africa.

The Bantu Authorities Act and the subsequent Bantu Self-Government Act of 1959 provided the lynchpin for grand apartheid, however, and from this developed the ambitious policy of Bantustans as separate and independent countries (see page 40).

! Simple essay style

Below is a sample exam question. Use your own knowledge and the information on the opposite page to produce a plan for this question. Choose four general points, and provide three pieces of specific information to support each general point. Once you have planned your essay, write the introduction and conclusion for the essay. The introduction should list the points to be discussed in the essay. The conclusion should summarise the key points and justify which point was the most important.

> How accurate is it to say that the purpose of the Bantu Education Act 1953 was primarily to prepare black Africans for unskilled jobs and a life of subservience to white South Africans?

﹖ Identify an argument   a

Below are a series of definitions, a sample exam question and two sample conclusions. One of the conclusions achieves a high mark because it contains an argument. The other achieves a lower mark because it contains only description and assertion. Identify which is which. The mark scheme on page 86 will help you.

- **Description:** a detailed account.
- **Assertion:** a statement of fact or an opinion which is not supported by a reason.
- **Reason:** a statement which explains or justifies something.
- **Argument:** an assertion justified with a reason.

> To what extent was the 1951 Bantu Authorities Act and 1959 Bantu Self-Government Act an attempt to give black Africans their own independent self-governing states?

Student 1

The 1951 Bantu Authorities Act and 1959 Bantu Self-Government Act were not really intended to give black Africans their own self-governing states. The 1951 Bantu Authorities Act said black Africans could only live permanently in their tribal reserves. Their leaders could be deposed by the South African government if they proved uncooperative. The 1959 Bantu Self-Government Act set up eight Bantustans, or homelands, from these reserves. However, many black Africans still lived and worked in white South Africa. The Bantustans themselves were poor and never able to become self-sufficient.

Student 2

The primary purpose of the two Acts was never really intended as giving black Africans their own independent self-governing states. They were more an answer to the conflict between the continuing need for a black African supply of cheap labour but unacceptability of allowing them to live permanently as citizens of South Africa. The Tomlinson Report of 1956 acknowledged that the homelands could never support more than two-thirds of their population and would need considerable investment to improve agriculture. Indeed it also recommended factories move just outside the borders of homelands so residents could commute across the border to work in them. The government was loath to accept these recommendations. Critics suggested the real purpose of the homelands was as a repository of cheap labour. They were not for example really independent: not only were they not going to be self-sufficient, but their leaders, appointed by the South African government, could be removed if they were uncooperative. This all suggests South Africa was going effectively to remain very much in control of them.

Political suppression and the Treason Trial

South Africa remained a democracy for white voters, and white opposition parties were tolerated so long as they were peaceful and did not attempt to recruit black Africans. However, any opposition from non-white groups was often brutally suppressed, and the security forces deployed both physical and psychological pressure. The main legal authority for repression in the 1950s was the Suppression of Communism Act in 1950.

Suppression of Communism Act, 1950

The government genuinely believed communist agitators were behind the majority of protest against apartheid. In suppressing communism too they were seen by the Western powers and USA in particular as a reliable ally in the Cold War.

Definition of communism

This Act defined communism as any scheme aimed 'at bringing about any political and social and economic change within the Union by the promotion of disturbance and disorder'.

- Communism was therefore a euphemism for any form of unrest, and the Act could be used to imprison anyone for anything the authorities deemed subversive.

- It could also ban organisations and individuals from contacting others for periods of up to five years by the use of banning orders. For many, this meant house arrest.

The British Lord Chancellor succinctly summed up the Act when he reported that anyone was a communist if the South African Minister of Justice said so.

The Communist Party after the Suppression of Communism Act

The CPSA dissolved itself and became an illegal organisation, the South African Communist Party, i.e. renaming itself. Its policy was that South Africa must become a non-racial state before communism could be successful there and therefore it continued to work with anti-apartheid groups, notably the ANC.

Other repressive Acts

The government also passed other repressive Acts:

- In 1953 the Public Safety Act allowed the government to call a state of emergency for twelve months in the first instance, with powers to renew it indefinitely.

- The Criminal Law Amendment Act of 1953 stated that anyone accompanying a person found guilty of a crime would automatically be assumed guilty too and have to prove their innocence.

- Censorship Acts in 1955 and 1956 aimed to prevent critical reporting and critical material being imported into South Africa.

- In 1956 the Riotous Assemblies Act outlawed any meetings which might engender hostility between the races, and prevent any 'banned' persons from addressing public meetings. This had been passed to prevent future meetings such as the 1955 Congress of the People, which had led to the Freedom Charter (see page 18).

The main intention was to isolate would-be protesters and prevent seditious material from reaching from their potential audience – with repression when it did.

The Treason Trial, 1956–61

Many different groups of all races had protested apartheid, and at a People's Congress in Kliptown in June 1955 drew up a Freedom Charter demanding equal rights for all in South Africa (see page 18).

Eighteen months after the ratification of the Freedom Charter, on 5 December 1956, the authorities arrested 156 of those who had attended the Kliptown meeting and charged them with high treason (conspiracy against the state). Those arraigned included the entire leadership of the ANC and most of that of the other opposition groups. After five months, they were accused of conspiring to overthrow the government and replace it with a communist regime. The ensuing Treason Trial dragged on for five years.

From 1957 onwards, some defendants were released for lack of evidence and indictments were withdrawn against 73 defendants. The trial against the remaining 30 defendants finally began in August 1959. While the defendants were in court, they could find little time for either covert activities or earning their livelihood. **Nelson Mandela** and **Oliver Tambo**'s law firm effectively went out of business during the trial.

In March 1961 the trial ended with the acquittal of all the defendants. The prosecution had failed to present a convincing case throughout the trial, and there was no evidence that any of the defendants had ever been guilty of treason. However, there was no sense of rejoicing. In South Africa, opposition groups were becoming more radical and the government was employing more oppression against them.

! Eliminate irrelevance

Below are a sample AS exam question and a paragraph written in answer to this question. Read the paragraph and identify parts of the paragraph that are not directly relevant to the question. Draw a line through the information that is irrelevant and justify your deletions in the margin.

How accurate is it to say that the government passed wide-ranging acts of suppression during the 1950s?

It would be very accurate to say that the government passed wide-ranging acts of suppression during the 1950s. The intention was to outlaw anti-apartheid movements. They did this primarily through the Suppression of Communism Act 1950. The regime hoped to equate anti-apartheid activity with communism, which was seen as a threat to the West during the Cold War. The Cold War meant war without fighting, in which the USSR and West were using international issues to engender one-upmanship on each other such as the Berlin Blockade and Airlift of 1948–49. By being tough on communism, South Africa hoped to prove itself a reliable ally with the West. However, the Act defined communism as any threat to political, economic or social order – in other words a very wide definition. Other measures reinforced suppression – such as the Censorship Acts in 1955 and 1956 to prevent critical material being imported into South Africa and the Riotous Assemblies Act to prevent any meetings which it was felt might engender hostility between the races, and preventing any 'banned' persons from addressing public meetings.

⚊ Spectrum of importance

Below are a sample exam question and a list of general points which could be used to answer the question. Use your own knowledge and the information on the opposite page to reach a judgement about the importance of these general points to the question posed. Write numbers on the spectrum below to indicate their relative importance. Having done this, write a brief justification of your placement, explaining why some of these factors are more important than others. The resulting diagram could form the basis of an essay plan.

'The measures taken to suppress anti-apartheid activity in the 1950s were highly effective because they were so wide-ranging.' How far do you agree with this statement?

- Measures taken to equate anti-apartheid activity with communism
- Banning orders
- Bans on meetings
- Vagueness of the wording of measures
- Wide-ranging types of measures
- Censorship to limit media coverage and importation of foreign literature
- The length of time of the Treason Trial and its impact on the defendants

←───→

Least important   Most important

African nationalism, 1948–59: Political opposition in 1948 `REVISED`

Africans and other non-white groups had protested about segregation and discrimination since the beginnings of South Africa.

African National Congress (ANC)

The main African opposition was led by the African National Congress (ANC). This had been formed in 1912 by a middle-class elite and had concentrated on debate and argument. However, it always supported campaigns to improve the lives of Africans and did attract grassroots (local) support.

South African Indian Congress (SAIC)

The SAIC had been founded in 1919 to support the promotion of rights of Indians and oppose segregation. It advocated passive resistance and sought to work with the ANC and other groups in a common front. To this end, an alliance was made with the ANC in March 1947: the so-called 'Three doctors' pact', as all the leaders had doctoral qualifications.

Communist Party of South Africa (CPSA)

The CPSA was a multi-racial party founded in 1921 with the aim of organising Africans into trade unions and uniting with white trade unionists on the basis of class rather than race. The CPSA often worked closely with the ANC, giving rise to the government accusation that the ANC leadership was itself communist.

The revival of the ANC

From 1940, under the leadership of Alfred Xuma, the ANC began to work more closely with other organisations such as the South African Indian Congress to develop a policy of non-cooperation involving civil disobedience. Again, it also developed support at local levels; for example, supporting the 1946 mine-workers' strike which saw as many as 100,000 on strike and brutal repression by the security forces. However, it was still seen largely as an organisation run by and for urban elites. Younger members were questioning the pace of its activities in comparison with the more direct action as exemplified by the unionists who were to organise the 1946 strike. In short, the ANC seemed to follow rather than lead developments in the struggle against apartheid.

The Youth League and the Defiance campaign

The pace of ANC activities and frustrations over its demands being ignored by successive governments led to the growth of more radical movements within the organisation.

In 1944 Walter Sisulu formed the ANC Youth League (ANCYL), which included a new generation of leaders such as Nelson Mandela, Oliver Tambo and **Robert Sobukwe**. The ANCYL sought a broader organisation with mass support. It emphasised the community-based culture of Africans which could be built on to promote mass action.

Africanism

Some leaders felt the ANC should only recruit Africans, while others, such as Mandela and Tambo, felt the ANC should effectively be multi-racial and welcomed support from all groups, notably the communists. This notion of Africanism was to be vital in the development of the anti-apartheid struggle.

The Basic Policy and Programme of Action

In 1948, partly as a response to the National Party electoral victory, the ANCYL created the Basic Policy which reflected three positions:

1 That Africans should unite as one group rather than members of different tribes.

2 That Africans had the right to the wealth and prosperity of Africa.

3 That Africans should accept the help of other sympathetic groups.

This was formalised in 1949 into a Programme of Action emphasising the need for direct action against apartheid.

The Defiance campaign

The Defiance campaign was the first large-scale example of direct action by the ANC. It was to be non-violent and divided into two stages:

1 An initial stage of local protest in which supporters would break the law, for example by refusing to carry passes and inviting themselves for arrest – the idea being that the sheer numbers of those arrested would exceed the authorities' ability to cope and also show the weight of opposition to apartheid.

2 Nationwide strikes and protests.

The campaign fizzled out because few Africans actually became involved and the government responded with suppressive measures. They also infiltrated anti-apartheid groups. The campaign was called off in January 1953.

The Freedom Charter

Most anti-apartheid groups came together in June 1955 to draw up the Freedom Charter, a statement of ideals and aims based on human rights such as equality before the law. However, critics saw certain clauses, such as advocating common ownership of the country's wealth, as supporting communism.

Quick quizzes at **www.hoddereducation.co.uk/myrevisionnotes**

Select the detail

Below is a sample exam question with the accompanying sources. Having read the question and the sources, complete the following activity:

How far could the historian make use of Sources 1 and 2 together to investigate how far the Freedom Charter offered a solution to the injustice of life under apartheid?

Below are three claims that you could make when answering the question. Read the claims and then select quotes from the sources to support them. Copy down the quotes on a separate piece of paper.

1 Black South Africans were treated unfairly.

2 The government was not based on the will of all the people of South Africa.

3 The Freedom Charter offered a blueprint for the future.

SOURCE 1

From Nelson Mandela's 'Spectre of Belsen and Buchenwald: Life Under Apartheid'. This article was written 5 October 1955.

Pernicious Face of Apartheid

The breaking up of African homes and families and the forcible separation of children from mothers, the harsh treatment meted out to African prisoners, and the forcible detention of Africans in farm colonies for spurious statutory offences are a few examples of the actual workings of the hideous and pernicious doctrines of racial inequality. To these can be added scores of thousands of foul misdeeds committed against the people by the government: the denial to the non-European people of the elementary rights of free citizenship; the expropriation of the people from their lands and homes to assuage the insatiable appetites of European land barons and industrialists; the flogging and calculated murder of African labourers by European farmers in the countryside for being 'cheeky to the baas'; the vicious manner in which African workers are beaten up by the police and flung into gaols when they down tools to win their demands; the fostering of contempt and hatred for non-Europeans, the fanning of racial prejudice between whites and non-whites, between the various non-white groups; the splitting of Africans into small hostile tribal units; the instigation of one group or tribe against another; the banning of active workers from the people's organisations, and their confinement into certain areas...

...the people's organisations have embarked on a broad programme of mutual co-operation and closer relations. The Freedom Charter recently adopted by people of all races and from all walks of life now forms the ground-plan for future action.

SOURCE 2

Extract from the Freedom Charter. The Freedom Charter was produced by representatives of many anti-apartheid groups in 1956 and offered a blueprint for a post-apartheid South Africa.

We the people of South Africa declare for all our country and the world to know:

- That South Africa belongs to all who live in it, black and white, and that no government can justly claim authority unless it is based on the will of the people.
- That our people have been robbed of their birthright to land, liberty and peace by a form of government founded on injustice and inequality.
- That our country will never be prosperous or free until all our people live in brotherhood, enjoying equal rights and opportunities.
- That only a democratic state, based on the will of all the people, can secure to all their birthright without distinction of colour, race, sex or belief.
- And therefore we, the people of South Africa, black and white together – equals, countrymen and brothers – adopt this Freedom Charter. And we pledge ourselves to strive together, sparing neither strength nor courage, until the democratic changes here set out have been won.

The Pan-Africanist Congress (PAC)

While the ANC still supported non-violence, other groups increasingly advocated an armed struggle against apartheid. This came to focus on rural protest and the formation of the PAC.

Action against apartheid

Rural resistance

The ANC admitted it had more support in urban areas – but during the 1950s there were many cases of rural unrest. These were often spontaneous and unplanned, making them more difficult to control or suppress.

Potato boycott, 1957 to 1959

This was an ANC-sponsored boycott of potatoes because of the harsh conditions endured by potato workers. Potatoes rot quickly, and stocks piled up as people refused to buy them. In August 1959 farmers began to improve working conditions and the boycott was hailed as a success.

Zeerust uprising, 1957

This uprising was precipitated by the imposition of passes for women living in the Zeerust area of western Transvaal, as introduced in the 1952 Native Laws Amendment Act. When the local chief was ordered to enforce this measure, he refused and was dismissed. The result was widespread protest. Men and women living in Johannesburg chartered buses to join the protest. These were subsequently arrested by the security forces and blamed for the unrest. The authorities were enraged when most were acquitted – but the women in Zeerust meanwhile were forced to carry their passes by a special police squad.

East Pondoland

The local chief of this region, who sided with the government, was accused of corruption. Local people insisted on his dismissal. As part of the protest locals boycotted white-owned stores. The chief survived, however, with help from the security forces, and the protests were called off in January 1961. Rural unrest and the lack of ANC influence in rural areas helped garner support for the newly formed Pan-Africanist Congress.

The formation of the Pan-Africanist Congress (PAC)

Robert Sobukwe had been an ANCYL leader but he disagreed with the **integrationalist** approach and was a firm supporter of Africanism (see page 18). In 1957 he helped form the Pan-Africanist Congress.

The PAC blamed the failures of the ANC on its willingness to work with other groups. In particular it rejected the Freedom Charter largely because of its emphasis on equal rights: many within the PAC rejected equal rights for whites who it accused of exploiting and oppressing black Africans. From its inception the PAC believed Africans could only act successfully by themselves. Many members – although not Sobukwe himself – saw whites as the enemy who must be expelled from South Africa. It also opposed communism, and associated itself with other independence movements in Africa, fighting colonialism.

The fundamental difference between the ANC and PAC was over the Africanist policy. The ANC insisted all racial groups could participate in the struggle against apartheid and all racial groups had an equal role to play in a post-society. Nor was the formation of the PAC a surprise: it had already expelled Potlako Leballo (see page 36) who was to become a key figure in the PAC, for his Africanist views.

Support

The PAC had a simple philosophy which was easily understood. It gained much support, especially in the Witwatersrand area, where many of its leaders were based, and in more rural areas. It has been estimated in fact that by 1959 its membership exceeded the ANC by as many as 25,000.

Differences between the ANC and PAC

ANC	PAC
Integrationalist – prepared to work with other racial groups.	Africanist – only prepared to work with Africans.
Saw the anti-apartheid struggle as unique – and realised any post-apartheid settlement must include whites.	Saw the anti-apartheid struggle as similar to other anti-colonial struggles in Africa.
Believed in equal rights for all racial groups – including whites.	Contained many supporters who saw whites as an enemy to be expelled from South Africa.
Prepared to work with communists and shared some communist ideas such as common ownership of wealth.	Opposed communism.

The PAC regarded itself as a rival to the ANC, and sought to pre-empt the ANC in the leadership of anti-apartheid activities.

(i) You're the examiner

Below are a sample exam question and a paragraph written in answer to this question. Read the paragraph and the mark scheme provided on page 86. Decide which level you would award the paragraph. Write the level, along with a justification for your choice, on a separate piece of paper.

How far could the historian make use of Sources 1 and 2 together to investigate the differences in ideas between the ANC and PAC?

The sources, taken together, show various similarities in the ideas of the ANC and PAC. Both agree that a priority must be to end white supremacy. Source 1 asserts that only when it is ended will national freedom be possible. Source 2 developed this idea by stating how black Africans are oppressed and degraded by apartheid. However, Source 2 goes on to state that Africans do not require help from other racial groups — the minorities — who they believe will attempt to dominate the struggle against apartheid. The ANC saw itself as a multi-racial organisation. It did not for example refuse help from white groups, notably communists. As a result Source 1 is of limited use in showing the differences as it does discuss this point — indeed from the extract one might suppose it is more anti-minority than the PAC, which assert all races should have a role in the new South Africa, including Europeans (by which they mean whites).

SOURCE 1

From the ANC Programme of Action, dated 17 December 1949.

The fundamental principles of the Programme of Action of the African National Congress are inspired by the desire to achieve national freedom. By national freedom we mean freedom from white domination and the attainment of political independence. This implies the rejection of the conception of segregation, apartheid, trusteeship, or white leadership which are all, in one way or another, motivated by the idea of white domination or domination of the white over the blacks. Like all other people the African people claim the right of self-determination. With this object in view, in the light of these principles we claim and will continue to fight for the political rights tabulated on page 8 of our Bill of Rights, such as:

1 The right of direct representation in all the governing bodies of the country – national, provincial and local – and we resolve to work for the abolition of all differential institutions or bodies specially created for Africans, viz. representative councils, present form of parliamentary representation.

SOURCE 2

From Robert Sobukwe's inaugural speech on the formation of the PAC in April 1959.

The Africans constitute the indigenous group and form the majority of the population. They are the most ruthlessly exploited and are subjected to humiliation, degradation and insult. Now it is our contention that true democracy can be established in South Africa and on the continent as a whole, only when white supremacy has been destroyed. And the illiterate and semi-literate African masses constitute the key and centre and content of any struggle for true democracy in South Africa. And the African people can be organised only under the banner of African nationalism in an All-African Organisation where they will by themselves formulate policies and programmes and decide on the methods of struggle without interference from either so-called left-wing or right-wing groups of the minorities who arrogantly appropriate to themselves the right to plan and think for the Africans.

We wish to emphasise that the freedom of the African means the freedom of all in South Africa, the European included, because only the African can guarantee the establishment of a genuine democracy in which all men will be citizens of a common state and will live and be governed as individuals and not as distinctive sectional groups.

Exam focus

On the following pages are sample exam answers to the questions on this page. Read the answers and the comments around them.

AS (a): Why is Source 1 valuable to the historian for an enquiry into National Party attitudes towards apartheid? Explain your answer using the source, the information given about it and your own knowledge of the historical context.

A-level: How far could the historian make use of Sources 1 and 2 together to investigate differing attitudes towards apartheid in South Africa? Explain your answer using both sources, the information given about them and your own knowledge of the historical context.

SOURCE 1

From pamphlet issued by the National Party Head Office in late 1947 ahead of the May 1948 election.

RACE RELATIONS POLICY OF THE NATIONAL PARTY

INTRODUCTION

There are two distinct guiding principles determining the South African policy affecting the non-Whites. One line of thought favours a policy of integration, conferring equal rights – including the franchise as the non-Whites progressively become used to democratic institutions – on all civilised and educated citizens within the same political structure.

Opposed to this is the policy of apartheid, a concept historically derived from the experience of the established White population of the country, and in harmony with such Christian principles as justice and equity. It is a policy which sets itself the task of preserving and safeguarding the racial identity of the White population of the country; of likewise preserving and safeguarding the identity of the indigenous peoples as separate racial groups, with opportunities to develop into self-governing national units; of fostering the inculcation of national consciousness, self-esteem and mutual regard among the various races of the country.

The choice before us is one of these two divergent courses: either that of integration, which would in the long run amount to national suicide on the part of the Whites: or that of apartheid, which professes to preserve the identity and safeguard the future of every race, with complete scope for everyone to develop within its own sphere while maintaining its distinctive national character, in such a way that there will be no encroachment on the rights of others, and without a sense of being frustrated by the existence and development of others.

AS (a): Why is Source 1 valuable to the historian for an enquiry into National Party attitudes towards apartheid? Explain your answer using the source, the information given about it and your own knowledge of the historical context.

Source 1 is valuable for an enquiry into National Party attitudes to apartheid because it was issued by the party shortly before the May 1948 election as a statement of their policy. The timing was apposite as many feared their rivals, the United Party, were about to soften attitudes to segregation. The source appears to confirm this without offering any evidence in support. However, it aims to win more electoral support for apartheid by condemning its alternative, greater integration. It offers a stark contrast between integration, which it sees as weak and disastrous for South Africa, and apartheid, which it asserts is in the interests of all racial groups.

Purpose of source explained but could be more on context.

Context of source explained.

However, it is also useful for showing the racist attitudes inherent in apartheid. While it states that apartheid would be in the interests of all groups, it emphasises that only apartheid is in the interests of the whites – in other words the democratisation implied by integration would effectively mean 'national suicide on the part of the whites'. Of course such democratisation would result in majority rule – an idea to which the National Party was absolutely opposed.

Content of source explained in terms of value.

The source also places apartheid within context – asserting it is a concept 'historically derived from the experience of the established white population of the country'. This of course refers to the segregation and policies of non-citizenship which applied to black Africans before 1948 – the 1923 Urban Areas Act for example. In this sense it shows apartheid as continuity rather than change and implies it is their rivals indeed who are seeking change through a policy of integration.

Uses own knowledge to support course content.

The source does have some limitations. It is a statement of intent: it does not say how apartheid could be implemented or indeed the varying degrees of apartheid. It does, however, suggest that there will be no encroachment of the rights of others. This shows the deep contradictions in the policy – by its very nature it must discriminate against other groups. It does imply white superiority by stating that apartheid would allow everyone to 'develop in its own sphere', with an implicit understanding that this means at their own level in the roles that are allocated to them. There is a sense that when at the end the source says, 'without a sense of being frustrated by the existence and development of others', this is referring to it being in whites' interests.

Shows limitations of value.

Shows the flaw in the argument.

Overall then the source is useful in showing why the National Party believes apartheid is preferable to all than what it sees as the alternative, integration. However, it is implicit throughout that it is primarily concerned with the interests of whites, the only voters.

Overall judgement on value with valid inference based on implicit meaning.

This is an accomplished response which interrogates the source well. It includes valid context and uses the information given. It offers a balanced view of the value of the source and would achieve Level 3.

Consolidation (sources) (AO2 & AO3)

These answers demand a combination of argument, own knowledge and reference to sources. Colour-code each of these three components.

SOURCE 2

From Nelson Mandela, Long Walk to Freedom. *Nelson Mandela became the first president of a democratic South Africa in 1994, after being a key figure in the ANC and imprisoned for years due to his anti-apartheid views and actions.*

Malan's platform was known as apartheid. Apartheid was a new term but an old idea. It literally means apartness, and it represents the codification in one oppressive system of all the laws and regulations that had kept Africans in an inferior position to whites for centuries ... The often haphazard segregation of the past three hundred years was to be consolidated into a monolithic system that was diabolical in detail, inescapable in its reach and overwhelming in its power. The premise of apartheid was that whites were superior to Africans, coloureds and Indians, and the function of it was to entrench white supremacy forever ... Their platform rested on the term baaskap, literally 'boss-ship', a loaded word that stood for white supremacy in all its harshness. The policy was supported by the Dutch Reformed Church, which furnished apartheid with its religious underpinnings by suggesting that Afrikaners were God's chosen people and that blacks were a subservient species. In the Afrikaners' world view, apartheid and the church went hand in hand.

The victory was a shock ... On election day, I attended a meeting in Johannesburg with Oliver Tambo and several others. We barely discussed the question of a nationalist government because we did not expect one ... I was stunned and dismayed but Oliver took a more considered line ... He explained, 'Now we will know exactly who our enemies are and where we stand.'

A-level: How far could the historian make use of Sources 1 and 2 together to investigate differing attitudes towards apartheid in South Africa in 1948? Explain your answer using both sources, the information given about them and your own knowledge of the historical context.

Both sources are valuable in investigating the different attitudes towards apartheid in South Africa. The first was issued by the National Party shortly before the May 1948 election as a statement of their policy. The timing here was apposite as many feared their rivals, the United Party, was about to soften attitudes to segregation. The source appears to confirm this without offering any evidence in support. However, it aims to win more electoral support for apartheid by condemning the alternative. It is then clearly a document aimed at winning votes – white electors of course being the sole electorate. It offers a stark contrast between integration, which it sees as weak and disastrous for South Africa, and apartheid, which it asserts is in the interests of all racial groups.

Introduces context.

Explains purpose of Source 1.

Source 2 opposes this view sharply. Mandela analyses the impact of apartheid on black Africans, showing the overt racism which underpinned it. He shows that it has already been present in variegated forms; the system now would consolidate and rationalise it. Mandela sees that the National Party victory would take segregation into a new all-embracing system – so the range and scope of apartheid would be extended as a result of the victory. He also recognised its purpose in maintaining white supremacy and shows how coloureds and Indians would suffer as a result of it too. He also introduces the Dutch Reformed Church which offers a religious underpinning of apartheid. In this sense Mandela sees an all-embracing system ostensibly as a God-given order. This offers succor to whites not only as the beneficiaries of apartheid but in the belief that it is a natural way of life.

Explains Source 2 in terms of contrast with Source 1.

Makes a valid inference.

Source 2 shows overtly the racist attitudes inherent in apartheid with its significance in entrenching white supremacy. While Source 1 would appear to disagree, stating that apartheid benefits all racial groups, its racism is more implicit. For example, it emphasises apartheid is in the interests of the whites – in other words the democratisation implied by integration

Quick quizzes at **www.hoddereducation.co.uk/myrevisionnotes**

would effectively mean 'national suicide on the part of the whites'. Of course such democratisation would result in majority rule – an idea to which the National Party was absolutely opposed. It also makes play of 'scope for everyone to develop within its own sphere while maintaining its distinctive national character' – a euphemism surely for unequal opportunities and belief that racial groups develop at differing levels. While attempting to argue the reasonableness of apartheid, Source 1 shows its inequalities and unfairness, reinforcing its inherent contradictions. Separate development means inequality as Mandela shows in Source 2.

> Comparative analysis of sources.

> Uses Source 1 to show the inherent contradiction in apartheid.

Both sources also place apartheid within context – Source 1 for example asserting it is a concept 'historically derived from the experience of the established white population of the country'. This of course refers to the segregation and policies of non-citizenship which applied to black Africans before 1948 – the 1923 Urban Areas Act for example. In this sense it shows apartheid as continuity rather than change and implies it is their rivals in the United Party indeed who are seeking change through a policy of integration. Mandela also sees apartheid as a system hundreds of years old, although he emphasises the change in range and scope that the National Party victory will bring. He also suggests a rationalisation. His colleague Oliver Tambo suggested that with the victory, things were clearer. 'Now we will know exactly who our enemies are and where we stand' emphasises again the consolidation of apartheid which the National Party victory presaged.

> Historical background.

Source 1 does have some limitations. It is a statement of intent: it does not say how apartheid could be implemented or indeed the varying degrees of apartheid. It does, however, suggest that there will be no encroachment of the rights of others. This shows the deep contradictions in the policy – by its very nature it must discriminate against other groups. It does imply white superiority by stating that apartheid would allow everyone to 'develop in its own sphere', with an implicit understanding that this means at their own level in the roles that are allocated to them. There is a sense that when at the end the source says, 'without a sense of being frustrated by the existence and development of others', this is referring to it being in whites' interests.

> Limitations of source utility.

Overall Source 1 outlines a policy which it suggests is in the interests of all groups although its implicit meaning suggests a goal of white supremacy to the detriment of other groups. Mandela has the foresight to see this, although he emphasises that apartheid already exists, albeit in less coherent forms. Mandela sees its evils while Source 1 records its strengths. Source 2 shows how blacks and other non-white groups are kept in subservience while Source 1 sees this more implicitly, particularly in the final sentence: 'without a sense of being frustrated by the existence and development of others'.

> Overall utility of each source.

This is a well-reasoned response which considers the utility of both sources both individually and together. Particularly impressive are the examples of comparative analysis where it is shown how they would agree and disagree with each other and the implicit nature of many of the comments as opposed to the overt in Source 1. The response demonstrates understanding of all the demands of the question. It would reach Level 5.

Consolidation

These answers demand a combination of argument, own knowledge and reference to sources. Colour-code each of these three components.

Peaceful protest

Protest about **apartheid** continued throughout the 1950s and early 1960s. In 1960, however, an event took place at Sharpeville which changed the nature of the protests to an acceptance of violence.

Peaceful protest had taken various forms such as strikes, boycotts and demonstrations but had achieved little:

- The government usually responded with repressive legislation. In 1956, for example, women protested about the extension of pass laws: the government passed the Native Administration Act which made it easier to remove Africans to their native reserves.
- Many anti-apartheid campaigners were too preoccupied with the Treason Trial to organise ambitious protests.

Nevertheless, the ANC called for a series of nationwide anti-**pass** protests to begin on 31 March 1960. The PAC decided to pre-empt this in its first show of strength.

The Sharpeville massacre, 1960

The PAC called for anti-pass protests throughout South Africa on 21 March 1960. While the overall response was disappointing, there was a sizable demonstration in the **township** of Sharpeville near Vereeniging. This was a centre of particular PAC support with all the usual problems of crime, high unemployment and associated social problems. It had a charismatic local leader in Nyakane Tsolo, and commuters were often pressured in supporting the protest rather than going to work that day.

The events of Sharpeville

On 21 March a crowd estimated to be as many as 20,000 gathered outside the police station at Sharpeville demanding to be arrested for not carrying their passes. The police couldn't arrest so many – although they did arrest PAC leaders – and there was a tense stand-off all morning. Triggered by events which are still disputed, at around 1 p.m. the police began to fire into the crowd: 69 demonstrators were killed, 70 per cent of whom were shot in the back as they attempted to flee.

Factors contributing to the massacre

- The authorities were on edge in the face of riots elsewhere, such as **Cato Manor**, and their senior officers were indecisive.
- It was a hot day and after hours of stand-off both protesters and police were tense.
- The police had arrested PAC leader Nyakane Tsolo, the one person who had seemed able to control crowd behaviour.
- The police were attempting to marshal the demonstrators into a nearby football field to manage them more easily and safely – but the demonstrators were reluctant, suspecting they were being herded into a killing field.

Aftermath

The shootings worsened the lack of trust between police and locals. To compound matters, police officers subsequently raged through the township, aggressively demanding to see passes, and even arresting the wounded in hospital. They insisted they had been under attack and presented two mounds of weapons and rocks as evidence for journalists. Locals meanwhile accused the police of placing weapons in the hands of the dead. It would be a long time before relations could be repaired.

The significance of the Sharpeville massacre

The Sharpeville massacre had great importance in the subsequent history of apartheid and protest against it:

- A state of emergency was declared on 30 March 1960, which saw thousands of arrests and the banning of anti-apartheid organisations (see page 28).
- The government appointed the Wessels Commission of Inquiry to investigate the events. While it accepted police leadership was indecisive it nevertheless exonerated the police of any blame, asserting that they acted in self-defence. It interviewed very few Africans and was inevitably accused of a whitewash.
- It served to make protest more radical and was instrumental in the decision of the ANC and PAC to turn to violence.
- The massacre caused international outrage, with widespread criticism from unfriendly countries and allies such as the USA. In Britain over 10,000 people protested outside the South African embassy. The UN called for the abolition of apartheid.

Add the context

Below is a sample exam question with the accompanying sources. Having read the question and the sources, complete the following activity:

> How far could the historian make use of Sources 1 and 2 together to investigate the reasons for the killings at Sharpeville on 21 March 1960?

First, look for aspects of the source that refer to the events and discussion that were going on around the time that the source was written. Underline the key phrases and write a brief description of the context in the margin next to the source. Draw an arrow from the key phrase to the context. Try to find three key phrases in each source.

Tip: Look at the information above the source – you should contextualise this too. Pay particular attention to the date on which the source was written.

SOURCE 1

From Africa South in Exile *Vol 4 No 4 July–September 1960, a magazine published in London. The magazine opposed apartheid and supported liberation struggles against colonialism throughout Africa.*

There are many who still doubt that the South African Government planned the killings at Sharpeville. Yet much larger crowds of protesting Africans than the one which assembled outside Sharpeville police station have since been dispersed with 3 warnings, baton charges, shots in the air or the wounding of a few front-line demonstrators in the legs. And surgeons giving evidence at the Sharpeville Commission of Enquiry claim that three-quarters of the Sharpeville wounded whom they examined in hospital had all been shot in the back. Eye-witness affidavits that no warnings were given by the police emphasize the significance of this. The Government decided upon a massacre at the outset of the anti-pass campaign, as the show of intransigence that it had for so long been promising the country. It is unfortunate that the show should have excited so much censure abroad, but no loyal Nationalist considers the show any less right or necessary than had the outside world ignored Sharpeville altogether.

A government capable of Sharpeville is unlikely to be turned from the highway of defiance it has chosen by the pluckings of protest. The censure of the outside world may be inconvenient; but white South Africa has suffered censure before, without feeling it necessary to make any changes in its conduct.

SOURCE 2

From Shooting at Sharpeville *by Ambrose Reeves, published in 1961. Reeves was Bishop of Johannesburg and a strong critic of apartheid.*

For what the police did at Sharpeville a heavy burden of guilt lies not only with Lieutenant Colonel Pienaar for his failure to control and superintend his men but also upon the individual policemen who fired. Standing orders also provide that the police must exercise great care that in firing they merely wound or maim their target and do not kill: at Sharpeville the police fired recklessly and indiscriminately into an unarmed crowd which was not attacking them. They killed 69 people and no justification or even extenuation can be found for such conduct ... At Sharpeville the police went on firing into the back of the crowd long after it had turned and begun to flee from the scene. They fired their automatic weapons in tremendous and devastating bursts and the only problem is to find suitable words of condemnation for the conduct of such an enormity.

Government reactions to radicalised resistance, 1960–61

In the two-month period following the Sharpeville massacre, a raft of repressive measures was passed.

State of emergency and the banning of political parties

- A state of emergency was declared on 30 March which saw the arrest of over 10,000 people, two thousand within the first few days. This number included **Nelson Mandela** and others who were still enmeshed in the Treason Trial.

- On 8 April, the PAC and ANC were declared illegal under the Unlawful Organisations Act. This was undoubtedly a blow for the ANC which hadn't been involved in the PAC campaign, although it was already preparing for an armed struggle. The forceful response by the government may have been because they were rattled; or alternatively because they sought to assert their authority and reassure investors and white citizens that they were fully in control. In the short-term period after Sharpeville there were indications of uncertainty among the white community which they needed to address.

Further repression

The new Minister of Justice, **John Vorster**, appointed in July 1961, instituted a new part-time Police Reserve Unit. This was to develop into the feared Security Police. He also set up secret, quasi-legal bodies to co-ordinate security matters and undertake 'dirty tricks' such as assassinations of opposition figures. These were to formally integrate in 1969 into the Bureau for State Security (BOSS) – but their activities remained state secrets.

Other measures followed:

- The Sabotage Act 1962 not only carried the death penalty for acts of sabotage but also placed the onus on the accused to prove themselves innocent; guilt was implied.

- In 1963 the General Law Amendment Act allowed the authorities to arrest anyone for 90 days without having to bring charges against them or even giving them access to a lawyer. Once the initial 90-day period was up it could be extended for a further 90 days and *ad infinitum*.

- The so-called 'Sobukwe clause' allowed the security forces to keep people in prison beyond the end of their sentence. Sobukwe was the first victim of it: he was imprisoned until May 1969 and then kept under house arrest: he was even denied proper treatment for the cancer which was to kill him in February 1978.

- Now that there was no effective check on their activities, the security forces increasingly resorted to torture to extract confessions, particularly through the use of electric shocks. This was allowed under the Sabotage Act of 1962.

- The authorities set a network of spies and informers to infiltrate opposition groups and if necessary to act as agent-provocateurs. These people were sometimes motivated by money, but also because they feared resistance to apartheid was useless and all Africans suffered for the actions of a few.

- In 1963 a new radio network was set up offering direct communication between over a thousand police stations and police headquarters in Pretoria to facilitate rapid response to incidents.

- The Bantu Laws Amendment Act 1964 came into effect on 1 January 1965. This empowered the authorities to deport any African from any urban area or white farming areas for any reason whatsoever. It also allowed the Minister for Bantu Affairs to establish quotas in particular areas or industries and deport unemployed Africans back to their homelands. This was a draconian (extreme) measure which gave the authorities complete power over Africans in 'white' South Africa. Anyone who caused problems, or it was felt had the potential to do so, could be removed.

⚡ RAG – rate the timeline

Below are a sample exam question and a timeline. Read the question, study the timeline and, using three coloured pens, put a Red, Amber or Green star next to the events to show:

● Red: events and policies that have no relevance to the question.

● Amber: events and policies that have some significance to the question.

● Green: events and policies that are directly relevant to the question.

> To what extent were the repressive measures passed in the period 1960 to 1965 a consequence of the Sharpeville massacre?

Now repeat the activity with the following questions:

> How far were government measures of repression in the period 1960 to 1965 a new departure from laws already in existence?

> What was the significance of the Sharpeville massacre on government attitudes towards protest about apartheid?

⚡ Develop the detail

Below are a sample exam question and a paragraph written in answer to this question. The paragraph contains a limited amount of detail. Annotate the paragraph to add additional detail to the answer.

> To what extent did government repression follow the Sharpeville massacre of March 1960?

The government responded to the Sharpeville massacre with a series of measures of repression. In April they declared a state of emergency. Some anti-apartheid groups were banned as a result. In the following year they passed a Sabotage Act. This was followed by the General Law Amendment Act in May 1963. The Bantu Laws Amendment Act was passed in 1964 to come into effect in January 1965. These were all responses to the Sharpeville uprising although the appointment of John Vorster as Minister of Justice in July 1961 may have had something to do with increasing repression too.

Creating a republic, 1960–61

Verwoerd's aims

Prime Minister **Hendrik Verwoerd** sought to create a totally apartheid state and the creation of a South African republic: he was opposed to the influence of Britain and to South Africa remaining in the **Commonwealth**, which he saw as increasingly dominated by newly independent African nations such as Ghana and Nigeria.

The significance of Macmillan's 'winds of change' speech

In February 1960, British Premier Harold Macmillan was touring Southern Africa and had been invited to address the South African parliament in Cape Town. As his audience looked on stony-faced, Macmillan made his famous 'winds of change' speech. He argued in essence that governments must accept the post-colonial changes in Africa and support them lest the newly independent nations turn to **communism**.

Vorster responded immediately to Macmillan's speech with a counter-argument that the whites in South Africa developed the country, made it prosperous and had the right to remain: he asserted that the whites of South Africa had nowhere else to go.

The South African government may have been disturbed by Macmillan's speech and indeed by the **decolonisation** going on throughout the continent. However, these developments would not deflect them from apartheid. Indeed, disastrous events – such those taking place in the former Belgian Congo where a bloodbath and civil war were raging – only served to confirm them in their path.

So while the 'winds of change' speech may have given encouragement to anti-apartheid groups, the government was firmly committed to the continuation of the system, and white control of South Africa; there would be no compromise. Moreover the debate, and increasing condemnation of South Africa within the Commonwealth, led to the creation of a republic independent from Britain.

The establishment of a republic

In October 1960, white South Africans went to the polls to decide whether they wanted to sever political ties with Britain and form a republic. With a 90 per cent turnout, it was a close call, with 52 per cent opting for republic status. Unsurprisingly, most support came from the Afrikaner heartlands of Transvaal and the Orange Free State: Natal had voted against the proposal, while voters in the Cape only supported it by 2000. Clearly there was to some degree a split between English and Afrikaans speakers.

Leaving the Commonwealth

It was perhaps inevitable that South Africa would leave the Commonwealth. In June 1961 Verwoerd attended his final Commonwealth Conference. He withdrew South African membership in the face of criticism over apartheid – although again it was a close-run thing; one of the main stumbling blocks to continued membership was Verwoerd's refusal to accept diplomats from newly independent African countries. It would, he said, lead to Pretoria being overcrowded with embassies. Privately, he acknowledged that African diplomats in an apartheid state could cause problems.

Relations with white Commonwealth countries

The withdrawal of South Africa from the Commonwealth did nothing to diminish its economic or cultural ties with Britain and the other white **dominions** such as Australia. One of the arguments of those who wished to retain ties was that trading links would be severed. This was not the case: economic and trading links continued to flourish while cultural links were maintained, particularly in terms of sport.

New Zealand and rugby

Of the white dominions, it was New Zealand which presented the most diplomatic problems as South Africa refused to allow Maoris (the indigenous people of New Zealand) to be included in visiting All Blacks rugby teams. The acquiescence in excluding the Maori players for the 1960 tour led to the biggest demonstrations in New Zealand's history. South Africa, however, did not care much, particularly if it meant their side had a greater chance of winning.

Chief Luthuli and the Nobel Prize

The president of the ANC **Chief Albert Luthuli** won the Nobel Peace Prize in December 1961. The authorities protested it was a bizarre choice but allowed the veteran anti-apartheid protester to attend the ceremony in Oslo.

South Africa had long retreated into a psychological **'laager mentality'** (see page 8) so it was not too concerned with international reactions – the 1960s was to see considerable economic growth, white immigration and the continued support and shelter of neighbouring countries.

Explain the difference

The following sources give different accounts of the challenges facing the apartheid regime in South Africa in the early 1960s. List the ways in which the sources differ. Explain the differences between the sources using the provenance of the sources, and the historical context. The provenance appears at the top of the source. Make sure you stay focused on the differences that are relevant to the question.

How far could the historian make use of Sources 1 and 2 together to investigate the challenges facing the apartheid regime in South Africa during the early 1960s? Explain your answer, using both sources, the information given about them and your own knowledge of the historical context.

SOURCE 1

From 'winds of change' speech by Harold Macmillan to the South African parliament, 3 February 1960. Macmillan was the British prime minister.

...the most striking of all the impressions I have formed since I left London a month ago is of the strength of this African national consciousness. In different places it takes different forms, but it is happening everywhere.

The wind of change is blowing through this continent, and whether we like it or not, this growth of national consciousness is a political fact. We must all accept it as a fact, and our national policies must take account of it.

Well you understand this better than anyone, you are sprung from Europe, the home of nationalism, here in Africa you have yourselves created a free nation. A new nation. Indeed in the history of our times yours will be recorded as the first of the African nationalists. This tide of national consciousness which is now rising in Africa, is a fact, for which both you and we, and the other nations of the Western world are ultimately responsible.

As I have said, the growth of national consciousness in Africa is a political fact, and we must accept it as such. That means, I would judge, that we've got to come to terms with it. I sincerely believe that if we cannot do so we may imperil the precarious balance between the East and West on which the peace of the world depends... As I see it the great issue in this second half of the twentieth century is whether the uncommitted peoples of Asia and Africa will swing to the East or to the West. Will they be drawn into the communist camp? Or will the great experiments in self-government that are now being made in Asia and Africa, especially within the Commonwealth, prove so successful, and by their example so compelling, that the balance will come down in favour of freedom and order and justice? The struggle is joined, and it is a struggle for the minds of men. What is now on trial is much more than our military strength or our diplomatic and administrative skill. It is our way of life. The uncommitted nations want to see before they choose.

SOURCE 2

From Prime Minister Verwoerd's response to Macmillan's speech, 3 February 1960.

The tendency in Africa for nations to become independent, and at the same time to do justice to all, does not only mean being just to the black man of Africa, but also to be just to the white man of Africa.

We call ourselves European, but actually we represent the white men of Africa. They are the people not only in the Union but through major portions of Africa who brought civilisation here, who made the present developments of black nationalists possible. By bringing them education, by showing them this way of life, by bringing in industrial development, by bringing in the ideals which Western civilisation has developed itself.

And the white man came to Africa, perhaps to trade, in some cases, perhaps to bring the gospel; has remained to stay. And particularly we in this southernmost portion of Africa have such a stake here that this is our only motherland, we have nowhere else to go. We set up a country bare, and the Bantu came in this country and settled certain portions for themselves, and it is in line with the thinking of Africa, to grant those fullest rights which we also with you admit all people should have and believe in providing those rights for those people in the fullest degree in that part of southern Africa which their forefathers found for themselves and settled in. But similarly, we believe in balance, we believe in allowing exactly those same full opportunities to remain within the grasp of the white man who has made all this possible.

African nationalist radicalisation, 1961–68

The period 1961 to 1968 saw a greater radicalism in African nationalism exemplified in particular by the movement to an armed struggle.

Moves to armed struggle

The Sharpeville massacre was simply one of a number of factors that led to the creation of the armed wing of the ANC, Umkhonto we Sizwe or Spear of the Nation (MK), in June 1961. The PAC had already created Poqo, their armed wing, whose activities were more militant still.

Government deceit

The government was as stubborn as ever and increasingly devious, for example arresting activists when they attended meetings with government officials.

Ineffectiveness of non-violent mass demonstrations

Opposition leaders finally realised that peaceful protest had never worked and was never going to work. When pass-burning became widespread, the police commissioner ordered the suspension of arrests for not carrying passes. However, Africans were told they could no longer draw pensions without their pass. Many were forced to queue to reapply for passes while their benefits were suspended.

The final peaceful protest

The ANC's direct action planned for 29 to 31 May 1961 failed. The government mobilised the army and police, ready for insurrection. The PAC meanwhile refused to participate because it was a multi-racial activity; they told their supporters to go to work as normal.

There was a poor response; few stayed home, fewer still demonstrated. This failure helped convince leaders that peaceful demonstration had finally had its day. This was the final peaceful mass demonstration of the 1960s.

Greater militancy among activists

The security forces had always been prepared to use violence. Anti-apartheid protesters were becoming increasingly militant and frustrated with peaceful tactics. Indeed, violence was widespread in many rural areas, for example in Eastern Pondoland where the rebellion led by the Intaba movement had been defeated by superior government forces and military hardware. The decision to begin an armed struggle was to some degree a case of leaders catching up with the demands of their supporters. The ANC remained conscious moreover that they had not been effective in rural areas and not given any military support to Intaba; the formation of an armed wing could eventually provide this sort of assistance in future conflicts.

The ANC and Umkhonto we Sizwe (MK)

Mandela co-founded the military branch of the ANC, Umkhonto we Sizwe (MK), in June 1961. Clearly it could not wage all-out war. It was decided that initially it would commit acts of sabotage on property such as government installations; the intention was to avoid loss of life. However, a second phase would involve volunteers training for guerrilla warfare. The overall aim, according to Mandela, was to make government impossible.

The beginning of Umkhonto we Sizwe (MK)

Much stress was laid on seeing MK as independent from the ANC. Members from the outlawed Communist Party, SACP and SAIC also joined.

MK began their campaign on 16 December 1961, to coincide with Covenant Day. Africans called this Digane Day, after the Zulu king who was defeated at the Battle of Blood River in December 1838. Bombings took place in government buildings in Durban and Port Elizabeth, including an electricity sub-station. In the next 18 months 200 attacks took place.

African Resistance Movement (ARM)

ARM was an armed offshoot of the white Liberal Party which was becoming increasing radical in its quest to abolish apartheid. While most of their members were arrested for sabotage by December 1964, their sentences were more lenient than for non-white groups, except for that of John Harris who was executed in April 1965 for a bomb attack at Johannesburg railway station which resulted in innocent deaths.

The PAC and Poqo

Poqo, the military wing of the PAC, was the most violent of the armed movements. It was far more prepared to operate using methods of terror and intimidation than the other groups and also targeted whites, whom it saw as an enemy. For example, it launched an assault on the town of Paarl on 22 November 1962, when a mob of 250 supporters armed with axes and home-made weapons attacked the police station and brutally hacked to death two young whites.

Eliminate irrelevance

a

Below are a sample exam question and a paragraph written in answer to this question. Read the paragraph and identify parts of the paragraph that are not directly relevant to the question. Draw a line through the information that is irrelevant and justify your deletions in the margin.

'The decision by the ANC leadership to turn to violence was largely in response to government repression.' How far do you agree with this statement?

The ANC leadership was increasingly frustrated by government repression which defeated peaceful protest. The government had passed a raft of measures in the early 1960s which banned protest and had outlawed groups such as the ANC. The security forces had always been prepared to use violence, for example in the massacre at Sharpeville, and activists were becoming increasingly militant and frustrated with peaceful tactics. At Sharpeville the authorities fired on peaceful protesters, killing 69 – although the authorities said the demonstrators were armed and threatening. Indeed, violence was already widespread in many rural areas, for example in Eastern Pondoland where the rebellion led by the Intaba movement had been defeated by superior government forces. The decision to begin an armed struggle was to some degree a case of leaders catching up with the demands of their supporters. There were, however, other factors such as the failure of peaceful protest. The government sometimes arrested leaders after they had agreed to meet with them. Accordingly MK began their campaign on 16 December 1961. Bombings took place in government buildings in Durban and Port Elizabeth, including an electricity sub-station. In the next 18 months 200 attacks took place.

Turning assertion into argument

Below are a sample exam question and a series of assertions. Read the exam question and then add a justification to each of the assertions to turn it into an argument.

To what extent was the decision among anti-apartheid groups to turn to armed conflict in the early 1960s a response to the failure of peaceful protest?

The ANC had decided to begin armed struggle in the early 1960s because
_____
_____

Peaceful protest had proved to be ineffective because
_____
_____

Many of their supporters believed the ANC leadership should have begun the armed struggle earlier because
_____
_____

Poqo was more extreme than MK because
_____
_____

In many ways the armed conflict was a response to the failure of peaceful protest because
_____

The Rivonia Trial and significance for Mandela

Capture of Mandela

After Nelson Mandela was acquitted after the Treason Trial, he went underground, working secretly, popping up at meetings and being known as the 'Black Pimpernel' because the authorities could not trace him. (The reference is to the Scarlet Pimpernel, the elusive hero of Baroness Orczy's novels set during the French Revolution.) He spent much time hiding at a farm called Liliesleaf in the Johannesburg district of Rivonia where he acted as a handyman; the farm was secretly owned by the Communist Party with whom MK (and the ANC) was in close co-operation. It was here that Mandela helped plan the formation and activities of MK.

Mandela spent some time abroad where he was trained in guerrilla warfare and lionised by supporters in cities such as London. However, in August 1962, on his return to South Africa, Mandela was arrested. He was accused of incitement to strike and travelling abroad without a passport. Grateful that he wasn't associated yet with MK, he realised defence was fruitless as the prosecution brought witnesses who could verify all the accusations. Therefore, he turned his defence instead into a further justification of the struggle. He was sentenced to five years in prison without parole.

The Rivonia Trial

While Mandela was in prison on the bleak Robben Island, on 11 July 1963 the security forces raided the Liliesleaf farm. Here they not only found MK operatives and caches of weapons but over 250 incriminating documents. Some of these appertained to Mandela's role; he had asked for them to be destroyed but they have been kept as valuable historical documents in a post-apartheid South Africa. Mandela therefore became the prime defendant in the Rivonia Trial, which began in October 1963. The trial attracted great publicity, was reported in many countries, and attracted large crowds each day mainly in support of the defendants.

The significance of the trial for Mandela

The guilt of the defendants was not in dispute. Not only did the prosecution offer the testimony of reliable informants but it had discovered papers relating to Operation Mayibuye, the plan for guerrilla warfare. The defendants realised there was little point in arguing a defence against the actual charges, but in open court they could justify their actions. The highlight of the trial was undoubtedly the four-hour speech by Nelson Mandela in which he admitted the charges that he belonged to the ANC and MK and again justified the ANC struggle against apartheid, calling for a non-racial South Africa.

Verdict

There was no question that the defendants would be found guilty. While they could have faced execution, the authorities had no wish to make them martyrs to the anti-apartheid cause. They were sentenced to life imprisonment. They were to be transferred to the Robben Island penal settlement where it was hoped in time they would be forgotten. The authorities believed they had defeated the most serious threat to the apartheid state.

International response to the Rivonia Trial

The Rivonia Trial attracted worldwide attention. The **United Nations** called for the defendants to be released while dockworkers in several countries threatened to refuse to handle South African goods in the ports. The new leader of the Soviet Union, Leonid Brezhnev, joined US Congressmen and British MPs in calling for clemency while 50 of the latter led a protest march in London. South African Premier Verwoerd claimed to have been unmoved by international protest. However, this opprobrium formed the context in which Judge Quartus de Wet had to deliver his verdict – and indeed the international concerns about the Rivonia Trial were significant reasons for the widespread protests against apartheid and sanctions against South Africa in the years to come.

Nelson Mandela's address at the Rivonia Trial, 20 April 1964

…we want equal political rights, because without them our disabilities will be permanent. I know this sounds revolutionary to the whites in this country, because the majority of voters will be Africans. This makes the white man fear democracy.

But this fear cannot be allowed to stand in the way of the only solution which will guarantee racial harmony and freedom for all. It is not true that the enfranchisement of all will result in racial domination. Political division, based on colour, is entirely artificial and, when it disappears, so will the domination of one colour group by another. The ANC has spent half a century fighting against racialism. When it triumphs as it certainly must, it will not change that policy.

⸬ Identify an argument

Below are a series of definitions, a sample exam question and two sample conclusions. One of the conclusions achieves a high mark because it contains an argument. The other achieves a lower mark because it contains only description and assertion. Identify which is which. See mark scheme on page 86.

- **Description:** a detailed account.
- **Assertion:** a statement of fact or an opinion which is not supported by a reason.
- **Reason:** a statement which explains or justifies something.
- **Argument:** an assertion justified with a reason.

'The main result of the Rivonia Trial was international condemnation of South Africa.' How far do you agree with this statement?

Student 1

The Rivonia Trial certainly led to international condemnation. However, it also showed government determination to defeat anti-apartheid activities and restore order. It believed a major trial would defeat the violence to which they had been subject by MK — 200 attacks in the 18 months following its formation in December 1961. The government wasn't concerned as a priority about international condemnation if it meant that MK would be defeated. However, international condemnation was acute and long-lasting: many leaders called for clemency and the international media interest brought South Africa into world focus.

Student 2

The Rivonia Trial took place in 1964. It was a result of the leaders of MK being captured. Notable among these was Nelson Mandela. Mandela knew he would be found guilty so used the trial to make a four-hour speech advocating democracy and equal rights in South Africa. This reached a worldwide audience due to media interest in the trial and was the main consequence. It led to international condemnation and caused protests in many countries.

ⓘ Developing an argument

Below are a sample exam question, a list of key points to be made in the essay, and a paragraph from the essay. Read the question, the plan, and the sample paragraph. Rewrite the paragraph in order to develop an argument. Your paragraph should answer the question directly, and set out the evidence that supports your argument. Crucially, it should develop an argument by setting out a general answer to the question and reasons that support this.

How significant was the Rivonia Trial on international responses to apartheid?

Key points

- The Rivonia Trial involved most of the ANC leadership.
- Nelson Mandela made a key speech justifying the struggle against apartheid.
- The trial was reported internationally and led to widespread criticism of South Africa.
- The leaders of many countries called for clemency.

Sample paragraph

The Rivonia Trial attracted worldwide attention. The United Nations called for the defendants to be released while dockworkers in several countries threatened to refuse to handle South African goods in the ports. The leader of the Soviet Union, Leonid Brezhnev, joined US Congressmen and British MPs in calling for clemency while 50 of the latter led a protest march in London. This opprobrium formed the context in which Judge Quartus de Wet had to deliver his verdict — and indeed the international concerns about the Rivonia Trial were significant reasons for the widespread protests against apartheid and sanctions against South Africa in the years to come.

The impact of exile and imprisonment on the ANC and PAC

By the early 1960s all the principal ANC and PAC leaders were arrested. Their activities diminished. It seemed that the government had been successful in its efforts to stifle protest and revolt. However, anti-apartheid organisations remained active, and were planning and preparing for future conflict.

The impact of defeat

Following the Rivonia Trial the structures of the ANC were all but destroyed. Its president, Chief Luthuli, was under house arrest and increasingly out of contact with colleagues. Many of its other surviving leaders, for example **Oliver Tambo** and **Joe Slovo**, went into exile in sympathetic African countries. Here they discussed future tactics while members underwent military training. Although there was a real desire to implement a guerrilla war against South Africa, the country was surrounded by friendly nations, making it extremely difficult to infiltrate guerrilla fighters within its borders. From the period 1963 to the end of the decade and indeed well into the 1970s there were no MK attacks within South Africa.

Alliance with ZAPU

In 1967 the ANC allied itself with ZAPU, an organisation fighting to destroy the white supremacist regime in Rhodesia. Although this led to good publicity for the ANC, the military results were limited. At best, ANC fighters received combat experience through involvement in the insurrection in the Wankie game reserve in Rhodesia. Overall, however, it had little or no impact on the capacity of the ANC to extend its struggle, as exemplified by the 1969 Morogoro Conference.

Morogoro Conference, 1969

This conference held in Morogoro, Tanzania, was intended to draw up a plan for victory and reform the structure of the ANC to facilitate this.

The main results of the conference were to re-emphasise the importance of the armed struggle within South Africa itself – at the time the ANC had no military presence there – and to give more voice to rank and file members. However, it would not be until the later 1970s and 1980s that the ANC really began to make its presence felt in South Africa itself.

The National Executive and Revolutionary Council

While the conference emphasised the multi-racial nature of the ANC, it stated that only blacks could serve on its highest body, the National Executive. The Revolutionary Council, however – which was to oversee the military struggle – was multi-racial. Members included white communists such as Joe Slovo whose links helped gain military supplies from communist countries such as the USSR.

PAC and Poqo

The PAC and Poqo fared even worse than the ANC in the 1960s. After the banning of political parties most of its leaders were arrested until Potlako Leballo emerged as the new leader from his base in Basutoland (now Lesotho). Leballo planned to organise a mass uprising in South Africa on 8 April 1963 in which whites would be indiscriminately killed. However, this was discovered: searches found the names of the entire membership of Poqo. Over 2000 supporters were arrested, effectively defeating the organisation. The PAC was riven with dissent and conflict until the resignation of Leballo in 1969. There was a short-lived friendship with China and a rebranding of Poqo as the Azanian People's Liberation Army in 1968, but overall it ceased to be significant in the struggle against apartheid.

Beginnings of Black Consciousness

In the absence of the ANC and PAC, new movements were taking shape which would come into fruition in the 1970s. With existing leaders in prison or exile, a new generation of activists were coming to the fore – many of whom were motivated by the **Black Consciousness** movement.

Black Consciousness was an international movement concerned in taking pride in black identity, history, culture and so on. Indeed in South Africa this manifested itself in a realisation among young Africans that the country offered them nothing and the purpose of education was to teach them they were inferior. In 1969 university students formed the South African Students' Organisation (SASO) to fight for better conditions and opportunities. This formed the germ of a wider protest movement in the 1970s dominated by the charismatic SASO leader **Steve Biko**.

Write the question a

The following sources relate to the ANC and PAC in exile in the 1960s and 1970s. Read the guidance detailing what you need to know about the impact of the ANC and PAC in exile during this period. Having done this, write an exam-style question using the sources.

SOURCE 1

From Henry Isaacs, 'PAC Activity in the Early 1970s', quoted in Tom Lodge, Sharpeville: An Apartheid Massacre and its Consequences, *published in 2011.*

Each morning the chief representatives and other assistants opened the office at 7.30. Senior PAC officials trooped in later to read the incoming mail, scrutinise invitations to conferences and if necessary nominate ... delegates to such conferences. Occasionally they discussed problems or read the *Tanzanian Daily News*. In the course of the day, PAC members filed into the office individually or in some groups. By noon the sparsely furnished office resembles a pass office in South Africa with inert humans everywhere waiting. They waited for the PAC Director of Finance to approve expenditure for 100 shillings for firewood ... There never was any bustle of activity or any sign of serious business ... After (lunch) almost everyone retired for an afternoon siesta.

SOURCE 2

ANC activist Joe Slovo describes the Morogoro Conference in The African Communist, *published in 1983.*

I want to say a few words about the Morogoro Conference. People tend to think about it loosely and for every person Morogoro seems to have a different meaning. Most people who talk about the Morogoro Conference tend to concentrate mainly on the integration of non-African revolutionaries into the external mission of the ANC. It is true that this was one of the key demands of the rank and file of MK (Umkhonto we Sizwe) and it was very hotly debated...

But Morogoro was more than this question alone. In the first place Morogoro asserted the right of the rank and file to have a say as to who would lead them...

Morogoro also proclaimed that we must devote the bulk of our resources to work inside the country [South Africa]. At the time the ANC's underground structures were virtually non-existent and MK had not fired a single shot on South African soil...

Looking back on it, comrades, it could be said there were moments at that Morogoro Conference when the very future of our whole movement seemed to be in jeopardy.

Strengthening 'separate development', 1961–68: Economic recovery

REVISED

The mid to late 1960s probably saw the apartheid regime at its most secure and confident. It was surrounded by friendly countries, opposition was largely defeated and many foreign interests were ready to invest in South Africa.

While the economy had suffered in the months following Sharpeville, with a reduction in foreign investment and a worrying level of emigration from professional whites who feared civil war, it was quick to recover in the wake of government repression and control.

Growth in Afrikaner prosperity

Traditionally the English-speaking whites had enjoyed more economic prosperity in South Africa but the 1960s saw a growth in Afrikaner wealth. They also took more management posts; for example, from 43.2 per cent of management and technical positions in 1948 to 68.1 per cent in 1960.

Percentage of Afrikaner ownership in industrial concerns

Industry	1948	1964
Mining	1	10
Manufacturing/construction	6	10
Professional	16	27
Finance	6	21

International investment

International investment grew, with many investors able to get 15 to 20 per cent return on their outlays. This investment stimulated the economy, with average economic growth of 6 per cent per year:

- The number of white people employed in manufacturing rose from 957,000 to 1,181,000 between 1960 and 1966.
- The white population itself rose from 3.09 to 3.77 million over the course of the 1960s, largely as a result of immigration.
- Per capita income among whites rose by almost 50 per cent during the 1960s, from R22,389 to R32,779.

British investment

Britain maintained close economic ties with South Africa – indeed British banks such as Barclays International controlled 60 per cent of South African bank deposits.

Diplomatic ties

South Africa emphasised both its anti-communist stance and position of stability in an increasingly unstable African continent. While many Western countries had anti-apartheid movements, their governments tended to value investments and ties more – few protested apartheid.

The USA also maintained close ties not least because it had extensive interests in South African minerals. While its leaders condemned apartheid, particularly during the Civil Rights era, they continued to see South Africa as a bulwark against communism and opposed sanctions: they also sold arms to South Africa to support its stance against communism.

Friendly neighbours

South Africa was surrounded by friendly countries, for example the Portuguese colonies of Angola and Mozambique and white-controlled Rhodesia. Even newly independent African nations such as Zambia relied on South Africa for trade and access to ports.

However, the South African economy had three fundamental problems:

1 It required considerable foreign investment.
2 It required the importation of heavy machinery and technical innovations, particularly in its mining industry.
3 It required the importation of all its oil.

In the 1960s these problems were all negated by the prevailing economic conditions. However, should any or all change, South Africa would be very vulnerable.

Life in white South Africa, 1961–68

Life for whites was generally good during the 1960s. They had access to plentiful economic opportunities, excellent social services, hospitals and education: many could afford at least one servant. Statistics of quality of life suggested white South Africans as a group were among the most comfortably off in the world. All statistics of health, education and life expectancy compared favourably with those in other developed nations.

However, whites rarely came into contact with other races outside master–servant relations. They were insulated if only through government control of media from the outside world: their education and experience taught them that apartheid was natural and non-whites were inferior. They were effectively living a lifestyle that was unsustainable.

The flaw in the argument　　　　　　　　　　　　　　a

Below are a sample exam question and a paragraph written in answer to this question. The paragraph contains an argument which attempts to answer the question. However, there is an error in the argument. Use your knowledge of this topic to identify the flaw in the argument.

To what extent did the South African economy recover from the international reaction to the Sharpeville shootings in the 1960s?

South Africa quickly recovered after the economic downturn following international reaction to the Sharpeville massacre although the economy was fragile because it relied on foreign investment. International investment, for example from Britain and the USA, grew with the result that more people were involved in industry, which grew by 7 per cent in each of the years of the 1960s. It was possible to expect 15 to 20 per cent profit on investment. The number of white people employed in manufacturing rose from 957,000 to 1,181,000 between 1960 and 1966. The white population itself rose from 3.09 to 3.77 million over the course of the 1960s, largely as a result of immigration.

 You're the examiner　　　　　　　　　　　　　　a

Below are a sample exam question and a paragraph written in answer to this question. Read the paragraph and the mark scheme provided on page 86. Decide which level you would award the paragraph. Write the level below, along with a justification for your choice.

How far was South Africa diplomatically and economically isolated as a result of international condemnation of the Sharpeville massacre?

While international condemnation continued after the Sharpeville massacre of 1960 and with the continuation of apartheid policies, the impact diplomatically and economically was slight. South Africa quickly recovered economically after the downturn following the massacre which saw for example reductions in foreign investment and increased emigration among whites. South Africa remained attractive to investors, with returns of as high as 20 per cent. This investment saw industrial growth with the numbers employed in manufacturing growing from 957,000 to 1,181,000 between the years 1960 to 1966. Western countries such as Britain and the USA were leading this investment: British banks in particular dealt extensively in South Africa. Diplomatically too, individual or group criticism did not lead to isolation – particularly as South Africa was seen as a reliable ally in the fight against communism. It was moreover surrounded by friendly countries – the Portuguese colonies of Mozambique and Angola and white-controlled Rhodesia for example. Even newly independent African nations relied on South Africa for trade.

Level:

Mark:

Reason for choosing that level:

_____

_____

_____

_____

Strengthening 'separate development', 1961–68: The impact on black Africans

Life for Africans was challenging. In 1980 one influential survey showed South Africa had one of the most unequal societies in the world: 10 per cent enjoyed 58 per cent of the national wealth while the lowest 40 per cent shared only 6 per cent. The lack of opportunities for Africans was exacerbated by the total apartheid policies pursued by the government.

Developing the Bantustans

The 1958 Bantu Self-Government Act laid the basis for the creation of eight **Bantustans**. This was not a new idea (see page 14). Afrikaners of extremist views had long suggested total separation of the different races, with Afrikaners themselves doing the unskilled work previously reserved for Africans. Prime Minister Verwoerd accepted the continuing need for permanent cheap African labour, but he was adamant there was no place for Africans in white society.

Verwoerd might also have been influenced by the decolonisation which was happening in Africa; Ghana had become independent from Britain in March 1957, Guinea from France in October 1958 and it was clear that other countries would shortly follow. The idea of Bantustans was a South African take on decolonisation. The African homelands currently governed as types of colonies; with tribal chieftains assisted by white officials, they would henceforth be prepared for full independence, to become fully self-governing and self-financing. Apartheid supporters could not understand how South Africa could possibly be accused of racism if this policy was pursued.

However, the homelands were based on the existing **tribal reserves**, which were still overcrowded and poor. Critics continued to see them as little more than repositories of cheap labour and dumping grounds for those not required. All the problems associated with the creation of Bantustans were immediately apparent in the first to become 'independent', Transkei.

Transkei

Transkei was the first Bantustan to be created in 1963 as a self-governing state (it received full 'independence' in 1976).

The leader of Transkei, Kaiser Matanzima, relied on coercion and declared a state of emergency which continued for much of the lifespan of Transkei. He attempted to prevent unrest and banned opposition groups through Proclamation R400, which had been issued to address the East Pondoland rebellions of 1960 (see page 20).

However, no other government recognised the Transkei and it was condemned by the United Nations and faced considerable unrest from the activities from Poqo, the military wing of PAC. Matanzima survived multiple assassination attempts but other chieftains weren't so lucky; for example, in October 1962 Poqo assassinated Chief Gwebindala Mabuza of the Tembo tribe.

Transkei never achieved anything like economic independence from South Africa and it continued much as before, as a reservoir for cheap labour. As an independent state, Transkei remained a sham, made up of three segments; a later Bantustan, Bophuthatswana, was made up of nineteen areas spread over hundreds of kilometres.

However well-intentioned Verwoerd was with the Bantustans policy, it clearly did not achieve its objectives and never won acceptance either outside South Africa or from opponents of apartheid within. Opposition moreover became more militant with the beginnings of violent protest and armed struggle.

Vorster's use of police powers and defence forces

Verwoerd's successor, John Vorster, had been a hardline Minister of Justice and continued to build up the police and defence forces: indeed, during his tenure as Minister of Justice, the defence budget had risen from R44 million to R255 million from 1961 to 1966. By 1970 South Africa had all the trappings of a police state.

Police powers

Police were given ever greater powers such as Section Six of the 1967 Terrorism Act, which gave them the ability to detain indefinitely anyone suspected of terrorist activities or of supporting them.

In 1969 the Bureau for State Security (BOSS) was created to co-ordinate the work of the defence and police forces. It reported directly to the prime minister; its activities were secret.

Defence forces

An Armaments Production Board was set up in 1964 to co-ordinate domestic arms production: R33 million was invested here. With the waves of measures of repression and power of the security forces, South Africa seemed on a war footing, perhaps an indication of how beleaguered it felt – despite the surface optimism.

Spot the inference (AO2)

High-level answers avoid excessive summarising or paraphrasing the sources. They instead make inferences from the sources, as well as analysing their value in terms of their context. Below are a source and a series of statements. Read the source and decide which of the statements:

- make inferences from the source (I)
- paraphrase the source (P)
- summarise the source (S)
- cannot be justified from the source (X).

Statement	I	P	S	X
Bantustans are economically unviable.				
Bantustans are simply a dumping ground for the surplus black African population.				
Bantustans are a fraud: they represent only 13 per cent of the land but are expected to sustain 80 per cent of the population.				
Bantustans are expected to sustain 80 per cent of the population but they are in the poorest areas and the government control the mineral rights.				
Bantustans comprise the areas white South Africans do not want because they are barren and infertile; however, should they contain wealth such as minerals these will be taken by the South African government.				

SOURCE

From Steve Biko, 'Let's Talk About Bantustans', undated essay in I Write What I Like, *a collection of essays first published in 1978. Biko was a Black Consciousness activist and leading anti-apartheid campaigner.*

Geographically, i.e. in terms of land distribution, Bantustans present a gigantic fraud that can find no moral support from any quarters. We find that 20 per cent of the population are in control of 87 per cent of the land while 80 per cent control only 13 per cent. To make this situation even more ridiculous, not one of these so-called 'Bantustan nations' have an intact piece of land. All of them are scattered little bits of the most unyielding soil. In each area the more productive bits are white-controlled islands on which the white farms or other types of industry are situated.

Economically the blacks have been given a raw deal. Generally speaking the areas where Bantustans are located are the least developed in the country, often very unsuitable either for agricultural or pastoral work. Not one of the Bantustans have access to the sea and in all the mineral rights are strictly reserved for the South African government...

Added to these observations is the fact that the operative budgets allowed the Bantustans for development projects are kept so low.

Recommended reading

- Peter Hain, *Sing the Beloved Country* (1996)
- Tom Lodge, *Sharpeville, An Apartheid Massacre and its Consequences* (2011)
- Francis Meli, *A History of the ANC: South Africa Belongs to Us* (1988)

Exam focus

Below is a sample A-level essay question followed by a model answer. Read the essay and the comments around it. Then tackle the task at the end.

To what extent did government suppression stifle anti-apartheid protest and rebellion in the period 1960 to 1970?

The government passed extensive measures to suppress anti-apartheid protest and rebellion in the 1960s, which resulted in most of the groups involved being outlawed and their leaders being exiled or imprisoned. Inevitably this reduced their ability to continue the struggle although as the decade developed new movements began to appear such as Black Consciousness, and exiled leaders continued to plan their future campaigns. However, overall the period saw government success in its battle against opposition.

> Makes a judgement which will be tested.

The initial event for escalation of government suppression in the 1960s was the Pass Protest campaign initiated in March 1961 by the PAC. The resultant Sharpeville shootings which left 69 protesters dead was followed by a raft of measures of suppression. A state of emergency was declared on 30 March which saw over 10,000 arrests. On 8 April, anti-apartheid organisations such as the ANC and PAC were banned under the Unlawful Organisations Act. This was succeeded by even more extensive measures of coercion, both legal and quasi-legal.

> Examines the types of suppressive measures.

In terms of the latter, the new Minister of Justice, John Vorster, appointed in July 1961, instituted a new part-time Police Reserve Unit. This was to develop into the feared Security Police. He also set up secret bodies to co-ordinate security matters and undertake 'dirty tricks' such as assassinations of opposition figures. These were to formally integrate in 1969 into the Bureau for State Security (BOSS) – but their activities remained state secrets. Effectively the impact of this meant the security forces were given licence to act as they chose without effective legal oversight. Now that there was no effective check on their activities, the security forces increasingly resorted to torture such as electric shock treatment to extract confessions, particularly through the use of electric shocks. The authorities set a network of spies and informers to infiltrate opposition groups and if necessary to act as agent-provocateurs.

> Explains how the security forces were able to operate so extensively.

These wide-ranging quasi-legal powers were supported by legislative measures. The Sabotage Act 1962 not only carried the death penalty for acts of sabotage but also placed the onus on the accused to prove themselves innocent; guilt was implied. The Act also allowed for coercion to exact confessions. In 1963 the General Law Amendment Act allowed the authorities to arrest anyone for 90 days without having to bring charges against them or even giving them access to a lawyer. Once the initial 90-day period was up it could be extended for a further 90 days and ad infinitum. The so-called Sobukwe clause allowed the security forces to keep people in prison beyond the end of their sentence.

By 1963 the ANC and PAC had adopted an armed struggle. Both had realised that peaceful protest was achieving nothing and the government was always ready to answer protest with violence and repression. Indeed the government was increasingly devious, for example arresting activists when they attended meetings with government officials. The final attempt at peaceful protest led by the ANC, strike action planned for 29 to 31 May 1961, failed dismally. The government mobilised the army and police, ready for insurrection. The PAC meanwhile refused to participate because it was a multi-racial activity; they told their supporters to go to work as normal.

The PAC had already formed its military wing, Poqo, which favoured guerrilla war, often targeting whites, as for example its assault on the town of Paarl on 22 November 1962. Nelson Mandela co-founded the military branch of the ANC, Umkhonto we Sizwe (MK), in June 1961. It was decided that initially it would commit acts of sabotage on property. However, a second phase would involve volunteers training for guerrilla warfare. However, the limitations of armed struggle were shown in East Pondoland where the superiority of the South African military was evident in its easy defeat of the Intaba resistance movement.

The leaders of MK were captured and put on trial – including Mandela himself. By the early 1960s all the principal ANC and PAC leaders were arrested. Their activities diminished. It seemed that the government had been successful in its efforts to stifle protest and revolt.

However, anti-apartheid organisations were far from dormant and were planning and preparing for future conflict. Surviving leaders of the ANC, for example Oliver Tambo and SACP activist Joe Slovo, went into exile in sympathetic African countries. Here they discussed future tactics while members underwent military training.

On the surface then, government suppression had been extremely effective in suppressing anti-apartheid opposition through its range, extensiveness and the wide powers given to the security forces. However, new movements were developing such as Black Consciousness, following the Black Power movement initiated in the USA. The exiled groups such as ANC continued to plan for the future – and the world was changing with the proliferation of independent African states and beginnings of insurrection in South Africa's Portuguese-controlled neighbours Angola and Mozambique. While government suppression may have been effective in the 1960s it could not control developments elsewhere and underestimated those in South Africa itself. They may have suppressed opposition in the short term, but it was still there and would reappear in new forms in the next decade.

Restores the analysis in showing how the potential for success in an armed struggle was limited.

Strikes a balance in terms of the question.

The conclusion summarises the points made and arrives at a valid judgement supported by evidence.

This essay addresses the issues and shows a wide range. It remains focused although there are some narrative sections. It is often difficult to avoid this but so long as the information is relevant and doesn't affect the analytical flow it shouldn't reduce the level. The conclusion is focused with a supported judgement. This essay should attain a Level 5.

Reverse engineering (AO1 & AO3)

The best essays are based on careful plans. Read the essay and the examiner's comments and try to work out the general points of the plan used to write the essay. Once you have done this, note down the specific examples used to support each general point.

AS questions

1 To what extent did the government suppress opposition in the 1960s?
2 'The ANC and PAC adopted a military campaign because peaceful protest had failed.' How far do you agree?
3 How accurate is it to say that the South African economy quickly recovered from the downturn following the Sharpeville shootings?

Steve Biko and the South African Students' Organisation (SASO) REVISED

In 1969 **Steve Biko** formed the South African Students' Association (SASO) as part of the **Black Consciousness** movement (see page 36).

Black Consciousness

Black Consciousness was tolerated by the government at first because they felt its emphasis on separate development might tie in with **apartheid**. Its goals included:

- non-cooperation with white groups, even those sympathetic to the ending of apartheid
- encouraging Indians and coloureds to see themselves as black and equally subject to white oppression.

The government soon turned against SASO because of its activities:

- In 1972 it organised strikes on university campuses about inferior facilities.
- In 1974 it celebrated the overthrow of the Portuguese colonial regimes in Mozambique and Angola, clearly seeing the struggle against the apartheid regime in South Africa in the same terms.

In 1973 Steve Biko was subject to a **banning order**: in 1975 SASO was itself banned. However, it continued as an underground organisation.

The mobilisation of school children

By the mid-1970s the education of black school children had reached a critical pitch:

- The reduction in government spending compounded by dramatic increases in the numbers of school children led to massive overcrowding: high school enrolment among Africans increased 150 per cent between 1970 and 1975, and class sizes in Soweto could be as high as 70.
- Schools lacked the resources to teach students the skills necessary to access any but the most menial jobs.
- In 1976, hardline Education Minister Andries Treurnicht insisted that half the lessons in African schools, including Maths, be taught in Afrikaans – a language that not all African children spoke and that was regarded as the language of repression.

The Black Consciousness movement had targeted children before, as in the 1973 strikes. School students were increasingly frustrated by the lack of educational opportunities and indeed an increasing awareness that the purpose of school was largely to keep them in servitude.

These factors led to a massive uprising in Soweto.

The Soweto uprising

Soweto was one of the biggest of the **townships**, with all the problems of overcrowding, squalor and crime. Problems in Soweto, as elsewhere by the mid-1970s, were exacerbated by the government's cutting subsidies on maize and corn at a time of economic downturn. However, Soweto also saw the creation of the school-based South African Students Movement (SASM) to campaign specifically against poor-quality education: it organised the Soweto protests.

In June 1976 there was a massive demonstration against the medium of Afrikaans in teaching in Soweto. Thousands of children took part and the protests spread to other areas in the Transvaal, Natal and the Cape. In a sense the teaching in Afrikaans was a final straw: children resented being taught in the language of their oppressors, in which many were not fluent. However, other more long-term factors should be considered too:

- The conditions in overcrowded townships such as Soweto – religious leader **Desmond Tutu** had warned the government three weeks earlier that anger was at crisis point. In Soweto, for example, it was common for as many as twenty people to share a four-roomed house with minimal sanitation.
- The conditions specifically in schools.
- The absence of recognised leaders who could possibly have marshalled their frustrations.

ANC leader **Oliver Tambo** was later to recognise that the ANC had few active units and no military presence inside Soweto, and communications between the exiled leadership and townships was poor. He did, however, assert that links were made wherever possible, citing activist Joe Gqabi, recently released from Robben Island, who worked with SASM, and was later assassinated by the security forces.

Following the outbreak in Soweto, the uprising continued throughout South Africa. Children went on strike, schools were burnt down, as were **shebeens,** which activists complained were taking the money which should have been spent in improving family life. The demonstrations and protest were the biggest seen so far.

Explain the difference

The following sources give different interpretations of education for Africans. List the ways in which the sources differ. Explain the differences between the sources using the provenance of the sources, and the historical context. The provenance appears at the top of the source. Make sure you stay focused on the differences that are relevant to the question.

How far could the historian make use of Sources 1 and 2 together to investigate the reasons for the uprising in Soweto in 1976? Explain your answer, using both sources, the information given about them and your own knowledge of the historical context.

SOURCE 1

Extracts from a Broederbund document justifying teaching black African children in Afrikaans.

- By far the majority of people in the Republic speak Afrikaans, 2.25 million whites plus 1.5 million coloureds ... against 1.25 million English speakers.
- Bantu workers make far more contact with Afrikaans speakers, for example in the mines, industry, farming, commerce, etc.
- Bantu officials and teachers mainly come into contact with Afrikaans-speaking officials and principals.
- Experience has shown that Bantu find it much easier to learn Afrikaans than English and that they succeed in speaking the language purely, faultlessly and without accent. There are even a few Afrikaans-speaking Bantu communities.
- Afrikaans is a language true to South Africa which for many reasons can serve the peculiar requirements of this country.
- White hospital personnel are mainly Afrikaans speaking.
- The police, with whom Bantu make a lot of contact, are almost all Afrikaans speaking.
- The white personnel of the railways are predominantly Afrikaans speaking.

The Broederbund also recognised African schools as strategic sites where Afrikaner hegemony could be implanted by using Afrikaans as a medium of instruction, observing in its September 1968 secret policy document:

- According to available figures about 3.5 million Bantu live on white farms ... English is seldom used on farms.

SOURCE 2

Extract from interviews with a teacher in an African school.

They were phasing out English as a medium of instruction. That in itself was confusion because they had the same teachers to teach them from Form 1 to Form 3. You can imagine if a person has to teach Form 1 in a different language, which is not a first language to that person, it's a second, third or whatever it is. And then also start teaching another foreign language, foreign in terms of it not being the mother tongue of the teacher for the same subject at another level ... How do you then deal with continuity, how do you then relate to your different classes ... what you were teaching and start reminding the student in Form 3, 'remember I started with this in Form 1, this is what I said' ... because now it's a whole language switch? So it wasn't just the problem that the students had. It was also the problem for the teacher. The teacher had to take through all these pupils and make a success of that and yet he or she had not been taught to use ... (Afrikaans) as a medium of instruction ... in terms of teacher training for secondary and high school ... The medium was English.

The authorities were taken by surprise at the strength of the initial demonstrations in Soweto. Then they responded with the usual brutality; police began to fire on the children, killing as many as twenty. The world was shocked by a photo showing the corpse of a thirteen year old, Hector Peterson. Nevertheless the authorities held firm. The Minister of Justice Jimmy Kruger blamed the demonstrators for fomenting trouble. Government officials accused them of seeking communist revolution while the official line remained that as the government provided the resources for African education it had the right to choose the form it would take.

The security forces may have killed as many as a thousand people as a result of these protests: **banning orders**, imprisonment and the suppression of eighteen organisations including the Christian Institute followed.

As the demonstrations continued it became apparent that no central organisation was directing them: not the ANC, PAC or even Black Consciousness. Most were localised, spontaneous and organised by school children themselves. This was a new feature in protest, more dangerous because of its unpredictability. Thousands of young people slipped away, to join armed groups preparing for **guerrilla warfare**. Government reaction to the Soweto uprising meanwhile led to widespread international condemnation.

The 'Committee of Ten'

The 'Committee of Ten' was formed in Soweto to organise a new system of local government in Soweto in which residents would vote for councils to run their affairs; the government rejected this out of hand.

People killed and injured by the police in the execution of their duties 1974–79 (not including those killed by police during the protests of 1976–77). Source: South African Institute of Race Relations

Year	Killed		Injured	
	African	Coloured	African	Coloured
1974–79	793	140	2024	478

The impact of the death of Steve Biko in 1977

Biko had been arrested in 1974 for breaking his banning order of 1973: he had attended rallies in support of the independence from Portugal of Angola and Mozambique. SASO itself was banned in 1975. Biko used his trial, in which he was a defence witness, to explain his case, attracting wide publicity and becoming an international figure.

Steve Biko died in police custody in September 1977. He was initially accused of attacking police officers during interrogation and falling against a wall during a violent struggle. A subsequent inquiry found he did in fact die of brain damage worsened by a 700-mile journey to a prison hospital covered only in a blanket. No one was prosecuted over his death.

The mysterious death of Steve Biko had great significance. It was not that Biko was the only victim of police brutality – the ANC recorded fourteen deaths in police custody in 1977 alone – but he was widely known about and widely respected abroad. He had in a sense become the face of black protest. His death in such horrific circumstances not only shocked many in South Africa but all over the world:

- Both the UN and USA protested over his death.
- There was widespread worldwide condemnation. He was to be the subject of a very popular movie, *Cry Freedom*, in the following decade, which led to even more international condemnation of the apartheid regime.
- The authorities remained impassive, as exemplified by Minister of Justice Kruger who asserted that Biko's death left him cold.
- An inquest reported improbably that Biko had gone berserk before fatally hitting his head against the wall. Few believed it.

The Soweto uprising and death of Biko marked the end of a point at which many people considered the chance of any peaceful solution to the problems caused by apartheid was possible. The government had spoken vaguely in August 1977 about giving coloureds and Indians more political rights but this had no impact at the time. It seemed a battle between an intractable and determined government and increasingly militant opponents of apartheid.

Add the context

Below is a sample exam question with the accompanying sources. Having read the question and the sources, complete the following activity:

> How far could the historian make use of Sources 1 and 2 together to investigate the significance of the Soweto uprising of 1976?

First, look for aspects of the source that refer to the events and discussion that were going on around the time that the source was written. Underline the key phrases and write a brief description of the context in the margin next to the source. Draw an arrow from the key phrase to the context. Try to find three key phrases in each source.

Tip: Look at the information above the source – you should contextualise this too. Pay particular attention to the date on which the source was written.

SOURCE 1

Extract from an editorial, 'The Will of an Entire People – Forged Under Fire', published in the magazine Sechaba *(Vol 11), published 1977.* Sechaba *is a magazine published by the ANC.*

These last months the South African people have mourned their heroic dead with their heads held high, their grief charged with pride and a renewed determination.

They are inspired by courage like that of the fourteen-year-old boy injured by buckshot in Soweto. He ran home for medical treatment and, despite his family's pleas, returned to join his comrades. It was his duty to continue the battle on the streets, he told them.

The minority regime is so savagely repressive that ordinary people are called upon to show extraordinary heroism in making their demands for the most elementary human rights. It has always been so for the masses. Time and time again they have shown more courage than it has taken for many a nation to gain independence, in other parts at other times.

The scale of the upsurge, its spread and persistence, since Soweto in June, is so great that it can be said to express the will of an entire people. A will forged under fire, too powerful and too clear ever to be effectively muzzled, divided or manipulated again.

SOURCE 2

From Nelson Mandela's response to the 1976 Soweto uprising, smuggled out of prison.

Unite! Mobilise! Fight on! Between the anvil of united mass action and the hammer of the armed struggle we shall crush apartheid!

In the midst of the present crisis, while our people count the dead and nurse the injured, they ask themselves: what lies ahead?

From our rulers we can expect nothing. They are the ones who give orders to the soldier crouching over his rifle: theirs is the spirit that moves the finger that caresses the trigger.

Vague promises, tinkerings with the machinery of apartheid, constitution juggling, massive arrests and detentions side by side with renewed overtures aimed at weakening and forestalling the unity of us blacks and dividing the forces of change – these are the fixed paths along which they will move. For they are neither capable nor willing to heed the verdict of the masses of our people.

THE VERDICT OF JUNE 16!

That verdict is loud and clear: apartheid has failed. Our people remain unequivocal in its rejection. The young and the old, parent and child, all reject it. At the forefront of this 1976/77 wave of unrest were our students and youth. They come from the universities, high schools and even primary schools. They are a generation whose whole education has been under the diabolical design of the racists to poison the minds and brainwash our children into docile subjects of apartheid rule. But after more than twenty years of Bantu Education the circle is closed and nothing demonstrates the utter bankruptcy of apartheid as the revolt of our youth...

While the Soweto uprising was organised locally, and spread largely unplanned to other parts of South Africa, it was felt that the traditional leaders of opposition to apartheid were becoming more irrelevant. However, the ANC was reorganising itself and preparing for a new phase of struggle.

Decline in the early 1970s

On the surface the ANC declined in importance in the 1970s. Its former leaders were still in prison, and the organisation itself was in exile. Many of those arrested after the Soweto uprising in 1976 initially treated people like Nelson Mandela with some degree of contempt when they met them in prison. They seemed relics of a previous age to those who had taken the initiative in protests in the absence of the ANC or PAC and were both more militant and ready to deploy violence. Many distrusted the **integrationist** policies and were more prepared to see all whites as enemies.

The ANC had not been involved in a military campaign since the unsuccessful Wankie uprising (see page 36). It seemed that the baton of rebellion had been passed on. However, Mandela and his colleagues were eventually to win over many of these new prisoners and indeed recruited them into the ANC. With those who had fled abroad they were to form the basis of the new generation of ANC activists.

Re-strengthening

Under the leadership of Oliver Tambo, however, the ANC was planning for a new phase of struggle. It was reorganised abroad to co-ordinate the following key activities:

● To oversee the growing number of exiles.
● To co-ordinate the activities of MK.
● To raise funds.
● To set up ANC offices throughout the world.

Within this there were frustrations, particularly among those who had left South Africa to be trained to fight. While the ANC maintained a growing number of military camps, it faced mutinies on at least two occasions when recruits grew angry about the lack of activities.

Centres

The ANC had headquarters in London where its strategies for gaining international support were mainly co-ordinated. It maintained forward bases in friendly African countries from whence it could launch raids into South Africa.

Visit to Vietnam

In 1978, ANC leaders visited Vietnam to study what it saw as its victory over the USA and success in uniting the country. As a result it changed tactics from attacks in rural areas to guerrilla warfare in urban areas, which it felt would carry more publicity. It saw its role as both military in terms of armed attacks and political in building up a mass organisation.

The biggest task for the ANC, however, was to make itself the clear leader of the opposition against apartheid. To do this it needed to win international legitimacy, to be seen not as a terrorist group but effectively as a government in exile.

External legitimacy

The ANC spent much of the 1970s winning external legitimacy, both in Africa and the wider world.

In 1963 the Organisation of African Unity (OAU) had been set up to encourage the newly independent African states to co-operate together: its Liberation Committee set up camps for ANC recruits and provided military training and equipment. However, African regimes were not strong enough to give more substantial support to the ANC; most traded with South Africa and some were dependent on it: Zambia for example was reliant on South African railways and ports to export the copper which comprised 95 per cent of its income. South Africa also placed pressure on regimes to expel the ANC, for example on Tanzania in 1969.

ANC leaders, e.g. Tambo, visited countries to try to win support and legitimacy. However, they were disadvantaged by being seen by many as pro-communist, particularly within the context of the Cold War, and having support from communist regimes. This was exacerbated by their close ties with the SACP.

Many groups and individuals in Western countries disliked the ANC stance on violence, typically asking them to stop the armed struggle; right-wing observers in Britain and the USA, for example, often regarded the ANC as a terrorist organisation. This limited their overall support.

Identify the concept

Below are five sample exam questions based on some of the following concepts:

- Cause – questions concern the reasons for something, or why something happened.
- Consequence – questions concern the impact of an event, an action or a policy.
- Change/continuity – questions ask you to investigate the extent to which things changed or stayed the same.
- Similarity/difference – questions ask you to investigate the extent to which two events, actions or policies were similar.
- Significance – questions concern the importance of an event, an action or a policy.

Read each of the questions and work out which of the concepts they are based on.

1 How far did the policies of the ANC leadership change after they went into exile in the early 1960s?

2 What was the significance of South Africa's wealth, geographical position and natural resources in terms of its relationship with other countries?

3 To what extent was South Africa's relationship with other countries the same in the 1970s as it had been in the 1960s?

4 To what extent was the ANC adoption of tactics of urban warfare a response to its failures in other spheres of activity?

5 How far was the lack of success of the ANC in the 1960s responsible for its reorganisation in the 1970s?

Develop the detail

Below are a sample AS exam question and a paragraph written in answer to this question. The paragraph contains a limited amount of detail. Annotate the paragraph to add additional detail to the answer.

How far did ANC policies and tactics change during the 1970s?

Many felt the ANC declined in importance in the 1970s. However, it was changing its policies and tactics. The ANC leadership in exile reorganised the organisation and gave it clear goals. These included overseeing the armed struggle, managing recruits and raising funds. However, there were frustrations among those who had volunteered to fight. The 1978 visit to Vietnam was important in terms both of military tactics and building up a mass organisation within South Africa. The ANC had also to maintain its position as the accepted leading group in the fight against the South African government. It did this by courting countries abroad. However, not all supported it. Many such as Britain and the USA were distrustful. Others in Africa were too reliant on South Africa economically to offer much effective support.

Oliver Tambo had been Nelson Mandela's law partner, and a fellow leader in the ANC. During the state of emergency in March 1960 he managed to escape and set up ANC headquarters in Dar es Salaam, Tanzania. Tambo effectively became the international 'face' of the ANC, its global ambassador. He remained its acting president until the death of **Chief Luthuli** in 1967.

Tambo's strategy

Tambo developed the two-pronged strategy of military conflict and the development of a mass political organisation, but progress was slow. However, he did keep the organisation intact and provided a unifying figure – for example, addressing the mutinies in which frustrated recruits sought to return to South Africa (see page 36).

Need for international support

Tambo saw in particular the need to build up international support and counter the accusations emanating from South Africa about the ANC's relationship with **communism**. To this end he would meet regularly with influential figures to explain the ANC position and assure where necessary that the ANC supported capitalist development; for example, he met with representatives of US multinational companies in the early 1980s in the face of President Reagan's aggressive stance against communism.

Making South Africa ungovernable

One of Tambo's biggest challenges was to keep the ANC unified while appealing to foreign supporters and indeed reassuring whites that they would have nothing to fear from an ANC victory. In January 1985, for example, in the face of **President Botha**'s state of emergency (see page 70), he advocated making the country ungovernable through military and non-cooperative actions. In October he also gave evidence to a British House of Commons committee which led to a British delegation being sent to South Africa to investigate the state of apartheid; their report was critical and supported sanctions.

Beginnings of guerrilla warfare

The ANC had begun to infiltrate guerrilla fighters into South Africa from the early 1970s. This was made easier after its neighbours won their independence and could be used as a springboard for attacks. However, one should not overemphasise this point. The ANC was never strong enough militarily to threaten the apartheid regime, although the persistence of conflict could weaken it in tandem with other factors, and did lead to a huge military commitment which drained the economy (see page 54).

MK attacks

MK attacks from the mid-1970s included sabotage of railways and industrial plants, attacks on government offices and assassinations, particularly of those accused of collaborating. Often they were planned to tie in with local concerns, such as an attack on a police station at Soekmekaar at a time when local people were angry about forced removals. Their strength was in their persistence rather than large-scale effect – although there was a rocket attack on a military base near Pretoria.

The global anti-apartheid movement

The ANC and other anti-apartheid movements gained considerable encouragement from the global anti-apartheid movement which covered many countries where people organised rallies and public events to show their opposition to the regime in South Africa. Governments themselves were often lukewarm, reluctant to offend South Africa, and wary of the ANC ties with communism and its military activities. There were exceptions: for example, India maintained close ties with the ANC and Scandinavian countries, particularly Sweden, provided aid and support.

Globally there were many active movements, such as the anti-apartheid movement in Britain in the 1960s, that promoted sanctions and boycotts, and there was encouragement from organisations in Holland and Canada. Popular support in the USA led Congress to impose sanctions in October 1986, overriding President Reagan's veto.

Select the detail

Below is a sample exam question with the accompanying sources. Having read the question and the sources, complete the following activity:

How far could the historian make use of Sources 1 and 2 together to investigate the development of the ANC military campaign in the period 1970 to 1985?

Below are three claims that you could make when answering the question. Read the claims and then select quotes from the sources to support them. Copy down the quotes on a separate piece of paper.

1 The ANC practised guerrilla warfare.

2 MK (the military wing of the ANC) has concentrated on economic and military targets.

3 The ANC campaign is having a serious impact on white South Africa.

SOURCE 1

Extracts from leaflets by the ANC distributed in South Africa.

Extract from a flyer distributed by 'leaflet bomb', commemorating Heroes Day, 15 December 1976, by the ANC:

'UMKHONTO provides our people with the skills of modern warfare. The bomb blasts and sabotage actions that rocked South Africa in the early 1960s are being heard again.'

Extract from a flyer distributed by 'leaflet bomb', commemorating the anniversary of Soweto uprising, June 1977, by the ANC:

The liberation movement, through Umkhonto we Sizwe, the armed wing of the ANC, has as its immediate task the launching of armed struggle in South Africa. In the mines and factories we must organise secret groups that will attack when the moment is right, through strikes, through sabotage, or other tasks which the liberation movement will call upon the people to undertake.

'Take the Struggle to the White Areas', distributed in South Africa in late 1985 by the ANC:

Forming underground units and combat groups in our places of work and taking such actions as sabotage in the factories, mines, farms and suburbs, and disrupt the enemy's oil, energy, transport, communications and other vital systems. Systematic attacks against the army and police and the so-called area defence units in the white areas.

SOURCE 2

From a confidential British Foreign and Commonwealth Office analysis of the ANC, dated August 1983, found in the Thatcher Foundation Archives.

1 The ANC's ultimate goal as set out in the Freedom Charter (1955) is a one-man one-vote unitary state based on socialist principles. Since 1960 the ANC has believed that this goal can only be achieved by violent revolutionary means. Its 'Strategy and Tactics of the South African Revolution' (1969) outlined the general principles and strategy of its armed struggle. Urban guerrilla warfare seems now to be the main element in this strategy.

2 The ANC has concentrated on guerrilla operations against economic and military targets in South Africa, infiltrating small groups of trained cadres from neighbouring states. Since 1977 nearly 200 instances of sabotage, clashes between police and guerrillas and assassinations have been recorded, most instances being attributed to the ANC. Economic targets have included fuel depots, power supplies, railway lines, the SASOP oil-from-coal plants and Koeburg nuclear station near Cape Town...

3 Although the ANC does not pose a direct threat to the survival of white South Africa, it has the capacity to erode white self-confidence by stretching manpower resources, causing significant economic damage and undermining a complacent lifestyle.

The National Party continued to win elections and be the party of government. However, as the 1970s progressed it faced more political challenges.

As society changed and South Africans became more aware of the wider world, there were two conflicting responses:

- A growth in liberalism particularly among the young; this manifested itself in the growth of the Progressive Party from one to seven MPs in the 1974 elections. This party advocated a federal structure for a non-racial South Africa. It renamed itself the Progressive Federalist Party when the old United Party collapsed in 1974, and became the official opposition in parliament. However, with 17 seats in 1977 as opposed to the National Party's 134, its impact was limited.

- Other whites became more entrenched, opposing any reform. They became associated in particular with Education Minister Andries Treurnicht, although they did not at present break away from the National Party.

Limited constitutional reform

Prime Minister **John Vorster** advocated reform in giving Indians and coloureds their own parliaments. The aim was to isolate black Africans further by bringing these two groups into limited power sharing. It was, however, too much too soon for hardliners who opposed the scheme. However, the government successes in the 1977 elections emboldened it to attempt limited constitutional reform. Although the Muldergate scandal and leadership change interrupted the process (see page 54), by February 1981 a separate President's Council made up of whites, Indians and coloureds was formed to advise the government, replacing the Senate. A separate black African Council had also been proposed but was shelved as no blacks were prepared to join it.

Problems in the Bantustans

The **Bantustans** meanwhile continued to fail. Four were granted full independence: Transkei in 1976, Boputhatswana in 1977, Venda in 1979 and Ciskei in 1981. However, none were recognised by any country other than South Africa. All were dependent on South Africa for subsidies: none were economically viable. By 1985 Transkei received 85 per cent of its income directly from South Africa.

Bantustans could not begin to support their official populations. In 1986 almost 250,000 Africans were arrested for **pass** offences. Most were classed as illegal aliens. One issue was that with developments in technology and indeed problems in the economy (see page 54), less unskilled labour was needed – indeed some white South Africans were being forced to take relatively unskilled jobs. As a result more Africans found themselves being deported. The Bantustans found their roles shifting from a repository for cheap labour to one where those no longer needed could be deposited.

Boputhatswana

Boputhatswana comprised nineteen separate areas of land hundreds of kilometres away from each other. It became the closest to attaining a degree of economic independence. This was largely because it contained an entertainment and casino complex, Sun City, which became a leisure centre for wealthy, mainly white South Africans as such venues were banned in their homeland. However, one should not exaggerate the economic impact. As many as 65 per cent of the population worked outside Boputhatswana.

Bantustan leaders

Bantustan leaders were largely unpopular and seen as collaborators. Typically, Bantustans remained dictatorships protected by South African forces. Hence, in 1988, they intervened to restore 'president for life' Mangope after an attempted coup. Nevertheless they didn't always oppose change, particularly when in Transkei in 1987, and Ciskei in 1990, the coups were against corrupt and venal leaders.

Developing an argument

Below are a sample exam question, a list of key points to be made in the essay, and a paragraph from the essay. Read the question, the plan, and the sample paragraph. Rewrite the paragraph in order to develop an argument. Your paragraph should answer the question directly, and set out the evidence that supports your argument. Crucially, it should develop an argument by setting out a general answer to the question and reasons that support this.

How accurate is it to say that Bantustans had no chance of successful development independent of South Africa?

Key points

- Although five Bantustans were given independence, none were recognised by any other countries.
- None of the Bantustans was economically viable.
- More unemployed black Africans were deported to them.
- Bantustan leaders were often seen as collaborators and they were politically unstable.

Sample paragraph

Five Bantustans were granted full independence: Transkei in 1976, Boputhatswana in 1977, Venda in 1979 and Ciskei in 1981. However, none were recognised by any country other than South Africa. All were dependent on South Africa for subsidies. Bantustans could not begin to support their official populations. More black Africans were deported to them. Bantustan leaders were largely unpopular and seen as collaborators. Typically, Bantustans remained dictatorships.

The flaw in the argument

Below are a sample exam question and a paragraph written in answer to this question. The paragraph contains an argument which attempts to answer the question. However, there is an error in the argument. Use your knowledge of this topic to identify the flaw in the argument.

To what extent did the ruling National Party face new political challenges during the 1970s?

The National Party faced two conflicting challenges during the 1970s. A growth in more liberal ideas particularly among the young: this manifested itself in the growth of the Progressive Party from one to seven MPs in the 1974 elections. This party, which grew, advocated a federal structure for a non-racial South Africa. It renamed itself the Progressive Federalist Party when the old United Party collapsed in 1974, and became the official opposition in parliament. Other whites meanwhile became more entrenched, opposing any reform. They became associated in particular with Education Minister Andries Treurnicht. These two opposing factors saw white politics becoming more fragmented and led to the National Party looking to widen the support base for the regime by introducing limited reforms to give coloureds and Indians some share in power and isolated black Africans even more.

As the 1970s progressed, the problems facing the National Party were compounded by scandals and economic challenges. By the end of the decade, moreover, the military commitment was becoming unsustainable.

Divisions and scandals in the National Party

The National Party was dividing into opposing wings, one of which favoured limited reform and the other a more conservative one which opposed all change. In the early 1980s, this was to split away to become the Conservative Party, while others formed even more extreme groups prepared to use extra-parliamentary violence to maintain apartheid.

Initially there were cosmetic devices to suggest reform while aiming mainly to satisfy the rival groups within the National Party. The name of the Department of **Bantu** Affairs was changed to that of Collective Development, while pejorative words in official government parlance were altered to cause less offence. 'Discrimination' for example became 'differentiation'.

It seemed, however, that having successfully emerged from the Soweto uprising and death in custody of Steve Biko, the biggest threats to the National Party came from within its own ranks.

In 1978 the National Party faced the so-called 'Muldergate' scandal in which large sums of money were discovered to have been syphoned off to pay for propaganda purposes:

- The publication of an English language newspaper, *The Citizen*, to support the regime.
- Bribes were distributed in countries such as the USA and Britain to promote the regime.
- Some funds were simply syphoned off for the perpetrators' own uses.

The scandal was focused around Minister of Information Connie Mulder who had been a potential candidate for prime minister when Vorster resigned in 1977: it was subsequently discovered that Vorster himself had been implicated, hence his prescient resignation. Mulder was associated with other senior government figures, thus threatening the very position of the government.

Impact on government

The state president, Nico Diederichs, died in August 1978. Vorster replaced him. This paved the way for P.W. Botha, the Minister of Defence, who was not implicated in the scandal, to become prime minister in September. In June 1978, a report discovered Vorster's involvement, forcing him to resign from the presidency.

Impact of 'Muldergate'

Mulder reluctantly resigned from the National Party. He went on to form the Conservative Party with other intransigents within the National Party. This was itself to become absorbed into the Conservative Party of South Africa formed by opponents of Botha's constitutional reforms (see page 68), which became the most significant opposition group in the 1980s – to the right of the National Party.

Economic pressures

South Africa faced increasing economic pressures. The costs of maintaining and subsidising the Bantustans were costly in themselves – but with the expense of defence added, the economy was struggling. This was in part due to the fluctuating price of gold in international markets, but South Africa, like most developed countries, suffered from huge increases in oil prices as a result of the 1973 **oil crisis**.

Standards of living

Part of the problem was that throughout the 1970s, GDP increased less than population so people as a whole were becoming poorer – including whites. Inflation was never less than 10 per cent – although it had more impact on blacks, it nevertheless hit whites hard. By 1977 more people were migrating from South Africa than coming in – and many of those who left were professionals. Indeed, the white population fell from 21 per cent of the whole at its peak in 1936 to 16 per cent by 1980.

The cost of defence commitments

South Africa spent 1 per cent of its GDP on defence in 1960: by the mid-1980s this had risen to 4 per cent, or 13 per cent of total government expenditure. The South African Defence Force (SADF) had doubled in size between 1960 and 1965, and continued to grow as its foreign commitments became more complex and widespread.

As South Africa's neighbours won their independence and turned from allies into hostility, its military commitments grew (see page 56). In August 1975 South Africa invaded Angola to try to impose its client organisation, UNITA, on that newly independent country. By 1977 military spending peaked at 5 per cent of GDP, with forces being deployed both externally and internally as a result of the Soweto uprising.

Establish a criteria

Below is a sample exam question which requires you to make a judgement. The key term in the question has been underlined. Defining the meaning of the key term can help you establish criteria that you can use to make a judgement.

Read the question, define the key term and then set out four criteria based on the key term, which you can use to reach and justify a judgement.

How accurate is it to say that political scandals were the <u>biggest threat</u> to the National Party during the 1970s?

Definition:

Criteria to judge the extent to which political scandals were the biggest threat to the National Party during the 1970s:

- _____
  _____
- _____
  _____
- _____
  _____
- _____
  _____

Reach a judgement

Having defined the key term and established a series of criteria, you should now make a judgement on the question above.

Summarise your judgements below:

- Criteria 1:

- Criteria 2:

- Criteria 3:

- Criteria 4:

Finally, sum up your judgement. Based on the criteria, to what extent were the political scandals the biggest threat to the National Party during the 1970s?

Tip: Remember to consider in your conclusion how far political scandals were the biggest threat in relation to other threats.

REVISED

By the mid-1970s, South Africa's control of its borders had become far more tenuous as former allies in the form of Portuguese colonies gained their independence and Rhodesia was gripped by a vicious war in which the black population were fighting to end white governance. The entire polity of Southern Africa changed. However, South Africa could maintain its economic influence.

Economic dependence

Longer-established states in Southern Africa may have protested apartheid but maintained ties with South Africa through economic necessity. Zambia, Malawi, Botswana and Swaziland, for example, all relied on South Africa for trade and egress to ports. Indeed, South Africa controlled oil and electricity supplies to these neighbours and employed their surplus workers: 280,000 in 1984. Efforts by these countries to co-operate to reduce their dependence on South Africa failed.

The impact of decolonisation

South Africa had relied on the Portuguese in particular for helping to control its borders to Angola and Mozambique. However, in 1974 the dictatorial regime in Portugal was overthrown and a new democratic government gave these countries their independence. South Africa became involved in their post-independence history in order to maintain this control. This was exacerbated in 1979 when a settlement in Rhodesia saw the creation of black majority rule in the renamed Zimbabwe.

South Africa's involvement in warfare

South Africa became involved in conflict with most of its neighbours.

Mozambique

In Mozambique the Marxist FRELIMO group took power, although South Africa joined with Rhodesia in offering support to its rival RENAMO – to little avail. Indeed, South Africa signed the Nkomati Accord in 1984. It agreed to stop supporting opposition groups in Mozambique if the Government there closed ANC bases.

Angola

South Africa's most significant involvement was in Angola where a civil war followed independence. Here it sided with the USA in supporting UNITA and indeed to that end launched Operation Susannah in October 1975. This was a major incursion which saw 3000 South African troops there by December. However, US support shrank, and South Africa was left isolated. It withdrew in July 1976, although continued to offer more covert assistance to UNITA. South Africa forces didn't finally withdraw until after the defeat at Cuito Cuanavale.

Battle of Cuito Cuanavale 1988

In 1986 Angolan government forces launched an offensive to destroy UNITA. South African forces came to their aid but were defeated at Cuito Cuanavale in 1988. After this they finally withdrew from Angola.

Namibia

South Africa had taken the former German South-West Africa as a mandate after the First World War and effectively governed it as a colony. By 1973 the United Nations declared this illegal. South Africa was in any event embroiled in a full-scale war with the independence movement SWAPO. This continued until peace negotiations took place in 1989 following UN Resolution 435, which had had proposed a ceasefire and UN-supervised elections. South Africa was accused of atrocities in Namibia, notably the attack on Kassinga refugee camp in May 1978.

Rhodesia

South Africa gave aid to Rhodesian forces fighting against independence groups. However, when Mozambique and Angola gained their independence, the South African government increasingly felt the Rhodesian regime was unsustainable, and began to concentrate their efforts, with little success, on convincing the white supremacist government to negotiate with more moderate black groups. In 1980 Zimbabwe became officially independent (see above).

The following sources relate to external pressures on South Africa in the 1970s, including its involvement in warfare. Read the guidance detailing what you need to know about external pressures during this period. Having done this, write an exam-style question using the sources.

SOURCE 1

From Hidden Lives, Hidden Deaths, *by Victoria Brittain, published in 1988. Brittain was a journalist specialising in events in West Africa. She is writing about the events at Kassala.*

The central force of every child's life is their response to what happened to them on 4 May 1978. A handsome boy at a desk at the back of the classroom volunteered to tell his story. 'It was early, about 7, and we were at the camp morning meeting before school when planes suddenly appeared and I saw bombs fall out of them. People began screaming and running and some bits of people were all around us on the ground. Then white soldiers shouting in Portuguese seemed to come from everywhere out of the bush...'

A journalist who arrived in Kassinga the day after the massacre wrote of the brightly coloured frocks of the young girls, jeans, checked shirts of the boys, a few khaki uniforms and swollen bodies of the dead. The victims were mostly very young and had no defence.

SOURCE 2

From 'Human Rights in Namibia', a paper given at the **Black Sash** *Annual Conference in March 1989. Black Sash was a women's group opposed to apartheid.*

...two major events in our history: the tenth anniversary of United Nations Security Council Resolution 435 and the tenth anniversary of the Cassinga (sic) massacre. Whilst both have something to do with the whole question of human rights, for Namibians the connection between these two events left a deep and painful scar. Not just because almost 600 Namibians died at Cassinga, but because the SADF raid on Cassinga refugee camp took place at the time when South Africa was in negotiations leading up to the adoption of Resolution 435 in August 1978...

The actions of the SADF at that time, of crucial importance, as an indication of the double-tracked strategy which formed an integral part of the policies South Africa was to pursue for the next ten years. On the one hand South Africa presented the façade of being ready to negotiate on Namibia's future whilst simultaneously creating obstacles to a negotiated settlement on Namibia's future by engaging in a wholesale aggression against the Namibian people and destabilisation of its neighbours.

International condemnation and call for economic sanctions

REVISED

South Africa was condemned internationally since the National Party victory of 1948. However, it was after Sharpeville and the **decolonisation** process in Africa that protest grew more vehemently. The regime did little to assuage this condemnation through its non-compromise policies.

The call for economic sanctions was widespread. In Britain, for example, the anti-apartheid movement originally focused on economic boycotts – it called for a month-long boycott of South African goods in March 1960, and for an international committee on sanctions to be held in Britain in April 1964. The UN had passed Resolution 1761 in November 1962, setting up a special committee against apartheid and calling for economic sanctions.

However, many Western counties refused to join this committee and as members of the **Security Council**, Britain, France and the USA had the power of veto, which they used to prevent sanctions becoming mandatory – the UN had for example called for an oil embargo as early as 1960, but this was not mandatory.

Western opposition to sanctions

We have seen that Western countries saw South Africa as a useful ally in the global struggle against communism. However, governments also argued that the regime might be more susceptible to reform if it remained part of the international community – if isolated it might become even more intransigent. Leaders also argued that, as they were the poorest group, sanctions would hurt the African population the most.

Arms embargo

The one area where sanctions became mandatory was over arms sales. The UN had called for a voluntary arms embargo as early as 1963 but it did not become mandatory until 1977 with Resolution 418 after widespread condemnation of the brutality with which the regime dealt with the Soweto uprising. However, other groups had made their own embargoes. For example, the 1971 **Commonwealth Conference** saw a resolution against arms sales and a projected deal by which Britain would supply helicopters and frigates was abandoned.

Impact of economic sanctions

Until the mid-1980s, economic sanctions, such as they were, had only a limited *economic* impact on South Africa, although they did add to the sense of hostility and isolation.

Reasons for limited impact

- We have seen (page 56) that countries in Southern Africa needed to maintain trade links with South Africa.
- Countries who wished to continue trading, notably Israel, could always get round sanctions.

US sanctions

During the 1980s significant opposition to apartheid grew in the USA, particularly as the fear from the USSR and communism diminished. We have seen that Congress overrode the president's veto over sanctions (see page 50). As a result more companies withdrew investment – 50 in 1986, 40 the following year – and, particularly seriously, US banks such as Chase Manhattan began to refuse to renew loans – for example, $10 million of short-term loans maturing in 1987. This created a severe financial crisis which led in part to the South African government beginning negotiations to end apartheid (see page 74).

One 1989 report estimated that, overall, economic sanctions had reduced the potential growth rate in South Africa by 10 per cent and cost 50,000 potential jobs.

Cultural and sporting boycotts

Cultural and sporting boycotts had begun in the 1960s with South Africa being suspended from the Olympic Games in 1964 and formally excluded in 1970. As a sporting nation, these boycotts were keenly felt. The **Commonwealth** passed the Gleneagles Agreement in June 1977 which forbade members to compete against South Africa: New Zealand faced considerable criticism when they invited the Springboks to tour in 1981. Generally, South Africa was isolated in terms of sporting and cultural links.

Nelson Mandela's 70th birthday concert

Opponents of apartheid realised the power of culture. The concert at Wembley to celebrate Nelson Mandela's 70th birthday in 1988 was broadcast in 67 countries and seen by an estimated 600 million people.

Support your judgement

Below are a sample exam question and two basic judgements. Read the exam question and the two judgements. Support the judgement that you agree with most strongly by adding a reason that justifies the judgement.

> How accurate is it to say that, by the mid-1980s, economic and cultural sanctions were having a major effect on South Africa?

Overall, economic and cultural sanctions had little effect on South Africa by the mid-1980s …

_____

_____

The withdrawal of US loans was the sanction that had the greatest effect on South Africa …

_____

_____

Generally, cultural sanctions had a greater effect on South Africa than economic ones …

_____

_____

_____

Tip: Whichever option you choose you will have to weigh up both sides of the argument. You could use words such as 'whereas' or 'although' in order to help the process of evaluation.

Spectrum of importance

Below are a sample exam question and a list of general points which could be used to answer the question. Use your own knowledge and the information on the opposite page to reach a judgement about the importance of these general points to the question posed. Write numbers on the spectrum below to indicate their relative importance. Having done this, write a brief justification of your placement, explaining why some of these factors are more important than others. The resulting diagram could form the basis of an essay plan.

> 'Economic sanctions damaged South Africa more than political condemnation or cultural and sporting boycott.' How far do you agree with this statement?

1 Impact of economic sanctions

2 Effects of cultural and sporting boycotts

3 Arms embargo

4 Political condemnation including from the USA

←——→
Least important   Most important

Recommended reading

- Steve Biko, *I Write What I Like* (originally published in 1978)
- Victoria Brittain, *Hidden Lives, Hidden Deaths* (1988)
- Alan Lester, *From Colonialism to Democracy*, Chapters 6 and 7 (1998)

On the following pages are sample answers to the questions on this page. Read the answers and the comments around them. Then tackle the activities which follow.

AS (b): How much weight do you give to the evidence of Source 2 for an enquiry into the value of sanctions in putting pressure on the South African government to reform apartheid? Explain your answer using the source, the information given about it and your own knowledge of the historical context.

A-level: How far could the historian make use of Sources 1 and 2 together to investigate the desirability of imposing economic sanctions on South Africa to end apartheid? Explain your answer, using both sources, the information given about them and your own knowledge of the historical context.

SOURCE 1

From Archbishop Desmond Tutu, 'Punitive Sanctions', a press statement dated 1986, published in The Rainbow People of God, *1994. Tutu is an influential and well-respected anti-apartheid campaigner.*

Nothing in South Africa, or very little has changed without pressure from the international community. The sports policy changed only as a result of the sports boycott which I have supported and continue to do so as a non-violent method to bring about change. I have called on the international community to exert pressure on the government, political, diplomatic, but above all economic pressure to persuade it to go to the negotiating table with the authentic representatives of all sections of our society...

Most Western countries have rejected economic sanctions because we are told these would hurt blacks most of all. I hope that most who use this judgement will just drop it quietly and stop being so hypocritical. It is amazing how everybody has become so solicitous for blacks and become such wonderful altruists. It is remarkable that in South Africa the most vehement in their concern for blacks have been whites. Very few blacks have repudiated my stance ... Even more remarkably two recent surveys have shown that over 70 per cent of blacks support sanctions of some sort.

SOURCE 2

Memo from the Prime Minister's Office to the Foreign and Commonwealth Office, concerning a meeting between Prime Minister Thatcher and South African opposition politician Helen Suzman on 2 August 1985, found in the Thatcher Foundation Archive. Suzman was a vocal opponent of apartheid who had been an MP since 1953 and had faced harassment by the security forces.

The general burden of Mrs Suzman's remarks was the South African government was much stronger than most people outside South Africa recognised. Moreover the majority of whites were not ready for one man one vote in a unitary state. Action to isolate South Africa or to impose economic sanctions would actually be counter-productive. But progress could be made by steady diplomatic pressure on the South African government on issues such as forced removals, abolition of pass laws and an end to attacks on neighbouring countries. She believed that the South African government was ready to make 'incremental changes' and Western governments should push for these. But one should not underestimate the advances which had already been made. One should recognise too that economic and industrial progress were the strongest forces for breaking down apartheid.

AS (b): How much weight do you give to the evidence of Source 2 for an enquiry into the value of sanctions in putting pressure on the South African government to reform apartheid? Explain your answer using the source, the information given about it and your own knowledge of the historical context.

Source 2 carries considerable weight into an enquiry into the value of economic sanctions at a time when there was heated debate as to whether sanctions should be applied. Its author is an opposition MP whose authority is clearly respected otherwise she wouldn't have been invited to talk with the British prime minister. Mrs Suzman makes several assertions on the basis of her expertise as a South African politician, which she presumably hopes will be useful to a foreign audience: that the South African government is stronger than most people outside South Africa realised, that most whites would not yet support democracy in South Africa, and economic sanctions wouldn't be effective. Mrs Suzman's voice offered a different view than many other opponents, for example Desmond Tutu who did argue for economic sanctions. The inference is that because of the present strength of the government and the intransigent of most whites, sanctions and attempts to isolate South Africa would only make them more entrenched in their views.

Question focus and some context.

Valid summary of argument and credentials.

Makes a valid inference.

Mrs Thatcher, with, for example, President Reagan of the USA, felt it was best to persuade the South Africans to change than attempt to coerce them. Her views therefore appear consistent with those of Suzman and may even have influenced her to maintain her stance against sanctions.

Suzman goes on to suggest the forms of international pressure that may be more effective – diplomatic for example, by which she presumably means persuasion, continued contact and dialogue. While others may consider this response weak, she nevertheless shares the criticisms of the apartheid state and its activities, listing forced removals, pass laws and incursions into neighbouring countries such as Angola and Namibia. Suzman has credentials as an opponent of apartheid, having been an opposition MP since 1953 and faced harassment by the security forces. However, she differed from many in her opposition to economic sanctions. Nevertheless again what she says appears consistent with Mrs Thatcher's stance of continued dialogue. Overall it seems that she told Mrs Thatcher what she wanted to hear. Others may have told her differently.

Possible impact of her views on her audience.

Clearly the source has limited weight in that the points are not substantiated – she asserts for example the strength of the South African government and views of whites without giving evidence in support. However, the nature of the source may be apposite here: a memo is a summary so what she said in full may have been compressed to offer a précis of her views. It is as it stands a summary of opinion, not necessarily fact.

Limitations of source.

Moreover this is one person's view and as it stands it lacks evidence in support. Others would give alternative opinions and offer evidence – for example, data on the impact of sanctions or the effects of sporting isolation. Suzman's opinion carries weight because of her credentials but other views might give a fuller picture as to the value of sanctions in pressurising the South African government.

This response is well-focused with valid analysis of the source. It explains its validity but also shows its limitations. It shows confidence in contextualisation. It distinguishes clearly between fact and opinion but also offers plausible reasons for this. This response should attain Level 4.

Consolidation (sources) (AO2)

It is useful to analyse sample answers such as this by colour-coding 'similarity', 'difference', 'own knowledge' and 'provenance'. This helps to recognise the relationship between each component part of the answer, and gives ideas on how such answers can be constructed.

A-level: How far could the historian make use of Sources 1 and 2 together to investigate the desirability of imposing economic sanctions on South Africa to end apartheid? Explain your answer, using both sources, the information given about them and your own knowledge of the historical context.

Both sources are useful in part in investigating the issue of whether or not to impose economic sanctions on South Africa although they hold conflicting views. Source 1 by Archbishop Desmond Tutu clearly advocates economic sanctions and indeed admonishes his audience for not imposing them, while Suzman feels they would be counter-productive. Both are opponents of the apartheid regime so they help illustrate the divisions within the anti-apartheid movement.

Shows understanding of question and the stance of source authors.

Source 1 comes from one of the most influential anti-apartheid voices in the 1980s. Archbishop Tutu's opinions carried considerable weight not just in South Africa but throughout the world. At a time when many were arguing against sanctions because they would harm blacks more than any other group, Tutu disagreed. He argued that the government had only ever responded to sanctions, for example sporting boycotts leading to some inclusion of non-white athletes in teams, and economic sanctions should therefore be applied.

Identifies the issue and author.

Context of source and purpose of author explained.

Tutu is quite impassioned in his arguments, calling those who reject economic sanctions hypocritical. The most vehement opponents of sanctions have been whites – because they argue they will hurt blacks the most. In Source 2 Suzman does not oppose them for this reason – rather that they will make the regime more entrenched in its opposition to change. However, he may have included her in his criticism of white opponents. Tutu uses evidence to show that blacks themselves support sanctions – in one survey over 70 per cent of those participating did so. Tutu clearly suggests here that the blacks' voice should be more influential than whites' over the desirability of economic sanctions. This is noticeable too in the first paragraph where he argues that economic sanctions would persuade the government to negotiate 'with the authentic representatives of all sections of our society', suggesting a validity for non-whites.

Comparative engagement with sources.

Explains source, showing evidence in support.

Source 2, however, disagrees. Its author is an opposition MP whose authority is clearly respected otherwise she wouldn't have been invited to talk with the British prime minister. Mrs Suzman makes several assertions on the basis of her expertise as a South African politician which she presumably hopes will be useful to a foreign audience: that the South African government is stronger than most people outside South Africa realised, that most whites would not yet support democracy in South Africa, and economic sanctions wouldn't be effective. The inference is that because of the present strength of the government and the intransigence of most whites, sanctions and attempts to isolate South Africa would only make them more entrenched in their views.

Makes a valid inference.

The reality was that sanctions had had only a limited impact hitherto because they were not mandatory. The UN had attacked apartheid every year since 1952 but Western governments had used their power of veto in the Security Council to reject compulsion. Economic sanctions were voluntary – but such was the wealth of South Africa in terms of minerals and natural resources that most countries chose to continue to trade with it. At the time Tutu was writing, their impact was limited because of their spasmodic nature. He does not suggest either any precise impact economic sanctions might have and upon which groups.

Makes a valid inference.

Mrs Thatcher, with, for example, President Reagan of the USA, felt it was best to persuade the South Africans to change than attempt to coerce them. Her views therefore appear consistent with those of Suzman and may even have influenced her to maintain her stance against sanctions.

Suzman goes on to suggest the forms of international pressure that may be more effective – diplomatic for example, by which she presumably means persuasion, continued contact and dialogue. While others may consider this response weak, she nevertheless shares the criticisms of the apartheid state and its activities, listing forced removals, pass laws and incursions into neighbouring countries such as Angola and Namibia. Suzman has credentials as an opponent of apartheid, having been an opposition MP since 1953 and faced harassment by the security forces. However, she differed from many in her opposition to economic sanctions. Nevertheless again what she says appears consistent with Mrs Thatcher's stance of continued dialogue. Overall it seems that she told Mrs Thatcher what she wanted to hear. Others may have told her differently. Clearly the source has limited weight in that the points are not substantiated – she asserts for example the strength of the South African government and views of whites without giving evidence in support. However, the nature of the source may be apposite here: a memo is a summary so what she said in full may have been compressed to offer a précis of her views. It is as it stands a summary of opinion, not necessarily fact.

Contextual information.

Inevitably both sources give one person's view, albeit someone with influence. However, neither gives alternative viewpoints – for example, what other means might be effective in getting the South African government to negotiate. Neither mention the impact of the arms embargo, in force since 1978, or what if any impact the sporting boycott had on South Africa as a whole.

Begins to strike a balance in terms of source utility.

Overall the sources have value to the historian because they do offer alternative viewpoints, although neither offer certainty that they are correct in those views. It might have been useful to offer more empirical evidence about the impact of economic sanctions. The sources are most useful in demonstrating that the anti-apartheid movement was not united – indeed Tutu may have called Suzman a hypocrite for her views. There was a variety of opinion as to the value of sanctions and the sources show the range of these.

Conclusion with judgement as to utility of sources.

This is a confident analysis of the utility of the two sources to the historian with valid comparisons and inferences. It is confident too in distinguishing between claim and information. Evaluation is valid with a concluding judgement. This essay should reach Level 5.

Consolidation (sources) (AO2 & AO3)

These answers demand a combination of argument, own knowledge and reference to sources. Colour-code each of these three components.

4 The end of apartheid and the creation of the 'rainbow nation', 1984–94

Revolt in the townships, 1984–87

By the mid-1980s, South Africa was in ferment with increasing violence and protest from the **grassroots** often uncontrolled by any central organisations.

The United Democratic Front

In August 1983, 575 organisations founded the **United Democratic Front (UDF)** whose aim was to co-ordinate internal opposition. Its ultimate goal was a new South African government based on the tenets of the Freedom Charter (see page 18). As part of this it sought the abandonment of the **Bantustans**, where many of its activities took place. The UDF came to be seen as the internal wing of the ANC.

Protest strategies

Support for the UDF may have been as high as 2 million. Many felt they were responding to **Oliver Tambo's** exhortation to make South Africa ungovernable (see page 50).

- It was particularly supported by the Indian Congresses and Congress of South African Trades Unions (COSATU). The number of strikes proliferated – and the number of days lost grew from 1,000,000 in 1986 to 6,000,000 in 1987.
- It organised marches, protests and demonstrations throughout South Africa. Local groups such as the Port Elizabeth Black Civic Organisation were affiliated and organised protests against poor housing and lack of electric supplies under its banner.
- In 1983 and 1984 it campaigned to get a million signatures for a mass petition against the proposed new constitution and black local government.

Black local government

As part of Prime Minister **Botha's** constitutional reforms, black Africans were given responsibility for the governance of **townships**. This led to huge problems because those choosing to participate were seen as collaborators and targeted by mobs. They also had to raise revenue by rent increases, which led to more unrest. Not surprisingly very few black Africans took part in the local councils.

Grassroots organisation

The UDF began a programme of 'People's Organs, People's Power', using local organisations to plan such activities as rent strikes and local courts to oversee communities. Indeed by 1989 rent arrears had grown to half a billion Rand. In 1983–84, Ciskei workers boycotted the buses taking them to work in the city of East London.

The advantage of these activities for the UDF was that there were no obvious national figures to arrest or ban: although in 1987 the UDF was banned, and many members were arrested, its activities continued – because there was no central organisation for the security forces to target.

The problem was that UDF-sponsored organisations were unable to stem a growing rate of violence.

Communal violence

Violence was getting beyond anyone's control. In 1984, in violent demonstrations against rent increases in the Pretoria-Witwatersrand-Vereeniging area, 175 people were killed. Many of the local courts descended into violence, with alleged malefactors being lynched or 'necklaced'. In 1985 alone over 800 people were killed as a result of political activity.

One concern was that different groups of Africans were turning on each other. In particular the Zulu group **Inkhata** emerged, claiming to be a national liberation group but increasingly responsible for black-on-black violence.

There had long been hostility between migrant workers who lived without their families in barrack-hostels and residents of the townships who favoured the ANC. In the 1980s this enmity escalated, particularly in Natal between supporters of the ANC and Inkhata. Because the latter tended to support the government more, they often had covert assistance from the security forces in their attacks on alleged supporters of the ANC.

Many feared that South Africa was descending into civil war. The townships in particular seemed uncontrolled.

Add the context

Below is a sample exam question with the accompanying sources. Having read the question and the sources, complete the following activity:

> How far could the historian make use of Sources 1 and 2 together to investigate the nature of the anti-apartheid revolt in the mid-1980s?

First, look for aspects of the source that refer to the events and discussion that were going on around the time that the source was written. Underline the key phrases and write a brief description of the context in the margin next to the source. Draw an arrow from the key phrase to the context. Try to find three key phrases in each source.

Tip: Look at the information above the source – you should contextualise this too. Pay particular attention to the date on which the source was written.

SOURCE 1

From 'Statement by UDF National Executive Committee on National Launching of UDF', August 1983. The UDF was an organisation to co-ordinate peaceful opposition to apartheid.

A declaration of policy and intent has evolved and is in the process of being finalised.

The conscience and the moral impulse of all freedom-loving people of South Africa have been aroused. People have been moved to reject these pernicious and evil laws which consolidate the heresy of apartheid.

Whilst the UDF articulates the viewpoint of the broad cross-section of people, we accept as fundamental that the main burden of exploitation and discrimination falls on the poor.

Accordingly, the main thrust of the organisation is directed towards the participation of working people in the workplace, in the communities and wherever they may be.

We call upon all democratic organisation to be directed towards the participation of working people in the workplace, in the communities and wherever they may be.

We call upon all democratic organisations who have not as yet identified with the UDF to join us and further unify the resistance to these new Bills.

The grand design of apartheid is to fragment our people's unity. And those who deliberately refrain from helping us to maximise this unity advance the cause of the enemy and delay the cause of democracy.

ISSUED BY: National Executive Committee of the United Democratic Front

SOURCE 2

From evidence given to the Truth and Reconciliation Commission by General M.A. Malan, Minister of Defence, 1980–90. The evidence is undated.

(c) Unrest-related statistics, September 1984 – April 1992: Unrest-related incidents 80,507; Persons injured during unrest-related incidents 18,061; Persons killed during unrest-related incidents 9,280

(d) Death or injury through burning in unrest-related incidents, September 1984 – December 1989: Death by necklace method 406; Injured by necklace method 28; Death by other burning 395; Injured by other burning 150

People were burned alive in the streets, bombs exploded in shopping centres and restaurants, innocent women and children died. The sight of dead and mutilated people was not uncommon. This was reinforced by threats from the neighbouring states that the struggle should be extended to white neighbourhoods. Once again, the actions of the members of the South African Defence Force should be judged against this background.

10.4 The psychological effect of the onslaught became visible in the community: homes with walls had steel gates added to them, schools were fenced with razor wire, security measures in public places were intensified and security personnel exercised access control in buildings and shopping centres.

Government suppression

The government itself added to the violence with its often brutal responses. In 1977, as Defence Minister, PW Botha had stated that South Africa was facing a **Total Onslaught** – a concerted attack by communist forces supported by the USSR. He believed this could only be combatted by a **Total Strategy**.

The Total Strategy involved the restructuring of government with the emphasis on security. Botha was helped in this in that he had been Minister of Defence for many years and had good relations especially with the Chief of the SADF, General M.A. Malan.

In 1979, Botha established a National Management System to oversee government: there were four cabinet committees in charge of policy: economic affairs, social affairs, constitutional affairs and security – with the last the most important.

State Security Council

Botha set up the State Security Council, comprised of army generals and police chiefs, to oversee security. It was supported at local levels by joint management committees. The police and armed forces therefore worked together, sharing information, planning joint operations and so on. The security forces were also involved in clandestine operations – for example, the assassination of activist Ruth First in 1982.

ARMSCOR

ARMSCOR was set up to bypass the world boycott on arms sales to South Africa. It developed the country's own arms industries.

Joint local management centres

These were tasked with gaining two types of intelligence:

- Hard intelligence, i.e. knowledge of plots and insurrections.
- Soft intelligence, i.e. ascertaining local grievances.

Overall, the Minister of Law and Order, Adriaan Vlok, summarised the aim of security policy as removing the activists while addressing grievances. It was therefore recognised that the two were closely connected and knowledge was passed on to organisations which could alleviate the latter. The police force itself numbered 50,000.

Government violence

The government was accused of brutal, often covert responses within South Africa. In 1987, for example, they were accused of bombing the headquarters of COSATU on the basis that it was used by members of MK. In 1987 the Civilian Co-operation Bureau was established to identify enemies of the state and security forces would then act – such as assassinating anti-**apartheid** critic David Webster in May 1989.

Many of the operations in which security forces were involved were covert:

- Crowbar was a special forces group founded in 1979, trained to fight SWAPO in Namibia.
- Government forces also infiltrated activists within South Africa, using spies and collaborators.
- Security forces opened fire on demonstrators – in 1986 as many as 500 blacks were shot dead by police.

The role of the security forces

The security forces became almost a state within a state. They carried out as many as 40 assassinations and made raids in neighbouring countries, including Angola, Lesotho, Mozambique and Zimbabwe. However, they were also operating within South Africa itself.

The security forces often gave help to vigilante groups who, later in the 1980s, were accused of responsibility for 90 per cent of unrest-related deaths. In 1985, one gang, the 'Phakatis', terrorised those supporting a schools boycott in the Orange Free State. In 1988 vigilante groups were blamed for the deaths of 1200 people in the Edendale Valley, a centre of unrest and ANC support in Natal.

Over time, the government became more effective at suppressing protest:

- More people were arrested and died in custody.
- It passed an Internal Security Act in 1982 by which anyone could be investigated and people banned without the need to give a reason.
- Censorship was extended: the Inquest Act of 1982 outlawed the reportage of deaths in custody and criticism of the security forces was banned under the Police Act.

Establish a criteria

Below is a sample exam question which requires you to make a judgement. The key term in the question has been underlined. Defining the meaning of the key term can help you establish criteria that you can use to make a judgement.

Read the question, define the key term and then set out four criteria based on the key term, which you can use to reach and justify a judgement.

How accurate is to say that the South African security forces became a 'state within a state' during the period of Total Strategy?

Definition:

Criteria to judge the extent to which the South African security forces became 'a state within a state':

- _____
  _____
- _____
  _____
- _____
  _____
- _____
  _____

Reach a judgement

Having defined the key term and established a series of criteria, you should now make a judgement on the question above.

Summarise your judgements below:

- Criteria 1:

- Criteria 2:

- Criteria 3:

- Criteria 4:

Finally, sum up your judgement. Based on the criteria, how accurate is it to say that the South African security forces became a' state within a state' during the period of Total Strategy?

Tip: Remember to weigh up how powerful and independent of government control the security forces had become in your conclusion.

Reasons for Botha's decision to negotiate, 1985–89

P.W. Botha, prime minister from 1978, was a former defence minister who maintained strong relations with the security forces. However, he recognised some change was necessary. His policy was to reform the political situation and indeed ease conditions for non-whites without sacrificing white supremacy. He was prepared to compromise on apartheid but not to share power. He saw this as a key part of the Total Strategy.

Reform

Botha knew the apartheid regime needed to be reformed to survive. He recognised black Africans were a permanent factor in townships and their hostility had to be assuaged. To this end many examples of petty apartheid were abandoned.

- The Mixed Marriages Act of 1949 was repealed in 1985.
- Local authorities were encouraged to desegregate parks and public amenities.
- **Pass** laws were abolished in 1986.

In addition, following the recommendations of the 1979 Wiehann Report, black trade unions were legalised.

The policy has variously been called WHAM – Winning of Hearts and Minds – and Adapt or Die. Nevertheless, Botha's main aim was still to maintain white supremacy. He felt this could best be achieved by 'divide and rule' – in other words including the Indians and coloureds in the political process, thereby separating them from blacks.

In 1984 a new constitution was introduced after a referendum of white voters accepted it by a two to one majority.

There was to be a new parliament, made up of three chambers:

- House of Assembly comprising 178 whites.
- House of Representatives comprising 85 coloureds.
- House of Delegates comprising 45 Indians.

In any joint sessions, it will be noted that whites could outvote the other two groups.

There would be a multi-racial cabinet responsible for 'general affairs', which meant issues such as taxation, defence, business and foreign affairs. Uni-racial ministerial councils were to be responsible for 'their own affairs', or education, health and local government, in so far as it applied to the separate racial groups.

Role of the president

The prime minister became president with executive powers – thereby increasing a role that had formerly been largely ceremonial. The president was:

- elected by a college of 50 voters, including 50 whites, 25 coloureds and 13 Indian MPs
- given the power to dissolve parliament at any time
- responsible for African affairs
- given the power to appoint a cabinet from members of all three Houses.

In addition the multi-racial President's Council (see page 52) was given the power to settle any disputes between the three Houses.

Criticism

Clearly the new system faced fierce criticism:

- Whites dominated.
- It maintained racial separation.
- The president was too powerful – for example, being able to dissolve parliament at any time.
- It was costly and overly bureaucratic.
- Africans were isolated, with no input. They were granted powers in local government (see page 64) but this created more problems than it solved. As a result, Indians and coloureds were at best lethargic and worst hostile – for example, only 30 per cent of coloured voters and 20 per cent of Indians voted in the elections. The constitutional reform was generally seen as a last-ditch attempt to maintain white supremacy.

However, the backlash from intransigent white politicians led to the formation of the Conservative Party of South Africa (see page 54).

Botha insisted in January 1985 that apartheid was outmoded and he welcomed an 'Eminent Persons' Group' of various **Commonwealth** heads of state to South Africa. He allowed them to meet with the imprisoned **Nelson Mandela** in March and indeed initiated government contacts with Mandela. At the same time government oppression continued and he intensified military activities against ANC and PAC bases abroad.

Changes in apartheid

Many still felt that Botha's reforms were largely cosmetic.

- The principal planks of apartheid such as the Population Registration Act remained in force.
- While much petty apartheid had been repealed, much still remained – for example, while buses had been desegregated, trains had not.
- More significantly, the townships where most black people lived still faced the same problems of overcrowding and squalor. Indeed, it was in attempting to improve these that the new black councils faced insurrection as a result of having to raise rents.

ⓘ Write the question   a

The following sources relate to President Botha's willingness to negotiate. Read the guidance detailing what you need to know about Botha's governance and the problems it faced during this period. Having done this, write an exam-style question using the sources.

SOURCE 1

From address by President P.W. Botha at the opening of the National Party Natal Congress Durban, 15 August 1985. This was known as the 'Rubicon Speech' because it suggested a large change of government direction.

The Party stands for the just and equal treatment of all parts of South Africa, and for the impartial maintenance of the rights and privileges of every section of the population. But, the Party must also deal with the heritage of history. Certain situations in this country were created by history and not by other national parties.

We are not prepared to accept the antiquated, simplistic and racist approach that South Africa consists of a White minority and a Black majority.

We cannot ignore the fact that this country is a multi-cultural society – a country of minorities – White minorities as well as Black minorities.

While the National Party accepts and respects the multi-cultural and poly-ethnic nature of South Africa's population, it rejects any system of horizontal differentiation which amounts to one nation or group in our country dominating another or others.

We believe in and uphold the principle of economic interdependence of the population groups as well as the acceptance of the properly planned utilisation of manpower.

SOURCE 2

From Zindzi Mandela, reading her father Nelson Mandela's response to being offered release from prison if he promised to renounce violence, from Nelson Mandela Foundation.

...But I cannot sell my birthright, nor am I prepared to sell the birthright of the people to be free. I am in prison as the representative of the people and of your organisation, the African National Congress, which was banned.

What freedom am I being offered while the organisation of the people remains banned? What freedom am I being offered when I may be arrested on a pass offence? What freedom am I being offered to live my life as a family with my dear wife who remains in banishment in Brandfort? What freedom am I being offered when I must ask for permission to live in an urban area? What freedom am I being offered when I need a stamp in my pass to seek work? What freedom am I being offered when my very South African citizenship is not respected?

Only free men can negotiate. Prisoners cannot enter into contracts. Herman Toivo ja Toivo, when freed, never gave any undertaking, nor was he called upon to do so.

I cannot and will not give any undertaking at a time when I and you, the people, are not free.

Your freedom and mine cannot be separated. I will return.

Economic problems

The South African government faced increasing pressures in the mid-1980s, resulting in the declaration of a new state of emergency in 1986.

The economic problems facing the state grew particularly as a result of US sanctions and the boycott by banks:

- In 1985 and 1986 over 90 US firms closed down their South African operations.
- In 1985 the international value of the Rand had fallen by 35 per cent and the stock exchange was in crisis.
- The cost of imports rose by 60 per cent between 1986 and 1987.
- In 1987 World Bank figures suggested South African growth rates would among the lowest in the developed world while inflation was the third highest among the industrial nations.
- Afrikaner businessmen were very pessimistic, fearing that investment would never return without meaningful reform.
- The white population was in decline while that of Africans rose exponentially, particularly in the cities. It was estimated that Africans would outnumber whites by five to one by 2000.
- Ironically, Africans as a whole were growing more wealthy, with the emergence of a new middle class. It was estimated that national percentage of disposable income for whites would fall from 55 to 42.5 per cent between 1985 and 2000.

Impact of international isolation

Botha's reforms did little to assuage international criticism. Many saw them as at best window-dressing. The continuing violence and brutality both on the part of the authorities and increasingly lawless groups added to the concerns.

According to a British Commonwealth Committee report, South Africa's policies abroad through intervention in neighbouring countries were responsible for:

- 1 million deaths
- 3 million homeless
- $35 million in damage.

By the time of the state of emergency, South Africa was more isolated than at any time in its history.

The failure of Botha's 'Total Strategy'

The aim of Total Strategy was to defeat the ANC and bring order back to South Africa. It failed for a variety of reasons:

- The economy was struggling, partly as a result of economic sanctions: inflation rose from 11 per cent in 1983 to 18 per cent by 1986.
- There was dissent within Botha's government – some wanted to maintain the military pressure, but it became apparent this was not succeeding. News of government operations only served to harden world opinion against South Africa and give support to opposition groups.
- There was no end to the violence in the townships.
- The security forces seemed unable to prevent the ANC and other groups committing acts of terror within South Africa – for example, attacking bars popular with members of the security forces. The number of incidents rose from 45 in 1984 to 281 by 1988.

The effect of the state of emergency

Botha declared a state of emergency in 1986. Its aim was to re-establish internal control, particularly over the townships. It also sought a lasting settlement within South Africa and continued domination over its neighbours. However, these ideas were no longer feasible unless the fundamentals of the regime were changed.

- The state of emergency did not remove underlying problems, which were now too great to control through coercion.
- The SADF deployed almost 8000 troops in the townships and committed acts of barbarism which by 1987 saw 43 admitted deaths in police custody, and as many as 29,000 arrests – but still the violence continued.
- Over 30 organisations, including the UDF, were banned. Media restrictions meant comparatively little went reported.

The main effect of the state of emergency was to turn South Africa into a dictatorship governed by coercion and suppression of information – but this had little impact on the problems it faced.

Spectrum of importance

Below are a sample exam question and a list of general points which could be used to answer the question. Use your own knowledge and the information on the opposite page to reach a judgement about the importance of these general points to the question posed. Write numbers on the spectrum below to indicate their relative importance. Having done this, write a brief justification of your placement, explaining why some of these factors are more important than others. The resulting diagram could form the basis of an essay plan.

How far was continuing unrest the main factor in the failure of the Total Strategy?

1 Continuing unrest despite extensive security measures

2 Economic factors

3 Divisions within the government

4 International condemnation

Least important ←——————————————————————————————→ Most important

You're the examiner

a

Below are a sample exam question and a paragraph written in answer to this question. Read the paragraph and the mark scheme provided on page 86. Decide which level you would award the paragraph. Write the level below, along with a justification for your choice.

How far were economic conditions responsible for the failure of the Total Strategy by 1987?

Economic problems certainly contributed to the failure of the Total Strategy. In 1985 and 1986 over 90 US firms closed down their South African operations. In 1987 World Bank figures suggested South African growth rates would be among the lowest in the world while inflation was the third highest among the industrial nations. Afrikaner businessmen were very pessimistic, fearing that investment would never return without meaningful reform. However, other factors were important too. The extensive security operations had failed to prevent unrest and the country was becoming more violent — despite the increasing costs. International criticism was growing, and South Africa was becoming increasingly isolated. It was the US banks' withdrawal of credit which caused a severe financial crisis but this was prompted by disapproval of US policies as reflected in the 1985 Anti-Apartheid Act. Indeed the causes are all interconnected. The cost of security operations added to pressures on the economy while the international condemnation led to the withdrawal of loans by US banks and business by US concerns. All these factors therefore worked together to bring about the failure of the Total Strategy rather than any   in isolation.

Level:

Mark:

Reason for choosing that level:

_____

_____

_____

_____

Negotiation and compromise, 1989–91: De Klerk's 'New Course'

P.W. Botha was incapacitated by a stroke in February 1989. In his first speech as president, his successor **F.W. de Klerk** outlined a 'New Course', which promised a real end to apartheid and power sharing between the different racial groups – but not integration as such.

De Klerk's New Course reflected the realities of the late 1980s:

- South Africa seemed on the verge of, if not already involved in, civil war.
- Economic decline continued.
- The National Party was losing support. Although it won the 1989 election it was with a reduced majority.
- Support from the USA and other Western countries diminished as **communism** was no longer seen as a threat.
- Influential business groups had pre-empted the New Course by already seeking dialogue with the ANC – for example, in Senegal in July 1987 three days of talks ended with a call for a negotiated settlement.

Elections to House of Assembly – three largest parties

Party	May 1987	September 1990
National Party	124	94
Conservatives	22	39
Progressive Federal Party 1987 / Democratic Party 1990	19	33

The New Course was effectively a statement that the government would work towards equal rights for all South Africans. It recognised the need to talk to opposition groups; to this end the ANC, PAC and SACP were legalised, and long-term political prisoners such as Nelson Mandela were to be released.

The significance of Mandela's release

Nelson Mandela was released on 11 February 1990 after 27 years in captivity. While others were also freed, his particular release was significant in the sense of his fame and symbolism as the victim of oppression in South Africa. People hoped he was the one leader with the charisma and dignity to facilitate a peaceful transition.

The government had been meeting with Mandela for some time to try to resolve the impasse: he had been offered his freedom as early as 1985 if he would renounce violence. He had met with government officials regularly, and while no agreement had been made with them, they had learnt to trust each other. He met with de Klerk in May 1989 and both men agreed to work together for a settlement.

The unbanning of political parties

The unbanning of political parties facilitated democratic elections once a settlement was reached. However:

- unbanning in itself had little effect on the violence and turmoil into which the country had descended
- it had little effect on political parties being ready to fight elections. The ANC, for example, had little formal political organisation within South Africa.

Problems for the ANC

The ANC faced dissent from within; many of those who had stayed in South Africa disagreed with the moderation of exiles whom they felt had had it easy. This was exemplified by the position of Mandela's estranged wife, Winnie, who was accused of involvement in murders of opponents.

- Many grassroots members of the ANC in fact had participated in violence and now it was difficult to control them.
- The ANC had been in exile for so long that it lacked internal organisation and administrative structures; these had to be quickly developed and suitably skilled and experienced staff found to run them.

It is important to realise that the National Party and ANC knew they had to work together to reach a lasting settlement and if they failed the result could be full-scale armed conflict. Their representatives met for the first time to begin negotiations in May 1990, and in August the ANC renounced violence. However, the talks were to proceed in a country which was becoming increasingly violent.

ⓘ Qualify your judgement (AO2)

Below is a sample exam question with the accompanying sources. Having read the question and the sources, complete the following activity:

How far could the historian make use of Sources 1 and 2 together to investigate the impact of F.W. de Klerk's speech of 2 February 1990?

Circle the judgement that best describes the value of the source, and explain why it is the best in the space provided.

1 Source 1 is valuable to a historian investigating the impact of F.W. de Klerk's speech of 2 February 1990 because it comes from the actual speech and the historian could analyse exactly what is being said.

2 Source 1 is of limited use because it comes from the speech itself rather than its impact.

3 Source 1 is partially valuable to a historian investigating the impact of de Klerk's speech because the historian can analyse exactly what is being said and use this in conjunction with other sources, which may explain the impact in terms of how dramatic a change it represents.

The best judgement about the value of Source 1 is _____

because _____

_____

SOURCE 1

From President F.W. de Klerk's inaugural speech, 2 February 1990. This speech advocated major reform in South Africa.

The steps that have been decided are the following:

- The prohibition of the African National Congress, the Pan-Africanist Congress, the South African Communist Party and a number of subsidiary organisations is being rescinded.
- People serving prison sentences merely because they were members of one of these organisations, or because they committed another offence which was merely an offence because a prohibition on one of the organisations was in force, will be identified and released. Prisoners who have been sentenced for other offences such as murder, terrorism or arson are not affected by this.
- The media emergency regulations as well as the education emergency regulations are being abolished in their entirety.
- The security emergency regulations will be amended to still make provision for effective control over visual material pertaining to scenes of unrest.
- The restrictions in terms of the emergency regulations on 33 organisations are being rescinded. The organisations include the following: National Education Crisis Committees, South African National Students' Congress, United Democratic Front, Cosatu, Die Blanke Bevrydingsbeweging van Suid-Afrika.

SOURCE 2

From Nelson Mandela, Long Walk to Freedom, published in 1994. Mandela was a leading anti-apartheid activist who became the first president of the post-apartheid South Africa.

On 2 February 1990 F.W. de Klerk stood before parliament to make the traditional opening speech and did something no other South African head of state had ever done: he truly began to dismantle the apartheid system and lay the groundwork for a democratic South Africa. In dramatic fashion he announced the lifting of the bans on the ANC, the PAC, the South African Communist Party and 31 other illegal organisations, the freeing of political prisoners incarcerated for non-violent activities: the suspension of capital punishment; and the lifting of various restrictions imposed by the state of emergency. 'The time for negotiation has arrived,' he said.

It was a breath-taking moment, for in one sweeping action he had virtually normalised the situation in South Africa. Our world had changed overnight. After 40 years of persecution and banishment, the ANC was now a legal organisation. I and all my comrades could no longer be arrested for being a member of the ANC, for carrying its green, yellow and black banner, for speaking its name. For the first time in almost 30 years, my picture and my words and those of my banned comrades could appear in South African newspapers. The international community applauded Klerk's bold actions. Amid all the good news, however, the ANC objected to the fact that Mr de Klerk had not completely lifted the state of emergency or ordered the troops out of the townships.

The impact of unrest and violence

The release of Mandela and unbanning of political parties had little immediate effect on slowing the violence which became the main factor in South Africa in the early 1990s.

No one seemed able to contain the violence between different African groups and which was frequently directed toward whites and other racial groups. Over 350 alone were killed on commuter trains between 1990 and 1993; often rival groups would ambush them as they crossed through 'their' territory.

Reasons for violence

- Many Africans had given up their education for rebellion during the 1980s and early 1990s and felt too unskilled to manage in a future South Africa.
- Many Africans remained suspicious of de Klerk – his party and government was still that associated with apartheid.
- There was a new mix – violent white groups and the creation of Inkhata, both of whom sought to maintain the status quo.
- The military wing of the PAC, the African People's Liberation Army (APLA), targeted whites as well as black opponents: they lost some support when in August 1993 they brutally murdered an American aid worker.

The role of Inkhata

The Inkhata Freedom Party was a Zulu group formed in 1990 by the Zulu leader **Chief Buthelezi**. Buthelezi was possibly the most important African leader within South Africa in the 1980s: he was prepared to work with the government and offered exemplary anti-communist credentials. With the unbanning of other groups and government talks with them, he saw his influence falling. Inkhata supporters began to attack those sympathetic to the ANC, particularly in the Zulu stronghold of Natal, and Buthelezi began to speak of secession from South Africa with a fully independent Zulu homeland.

White extremist reaction

Many whites opposed the changes taking place. Some were prepared to work democratically through the Conservative Party but others supported violence. The Afrikaner Weerstandsbeweging (AWB) threatened violence and indeed committed bombings and acts of intimidation; it also sought to prevent negotiations by storming the hall where meetings were being held. The AWB sought an independent white homeland.

The growth in numbers of poor whites

Many whites had suffered economically with the appearance of more skilled non-whites in the workforce and the dismantling of an apartheid system which often protected their jobs. In 1991 hunger relief agencies were estimated to support over 20,000 whites. This group proved a fertile recruiting ground for white extremist groups.

The dismantling of apartheid

Many were surprised by the extent of de Klerk's February 1990 speech. They were expecting it to focus on the release of Mandela – but it was in fact that speech which formally committed the government to constitutional change.

- In October 1990 the Separate Amenities Act which had formed the basis for petty apartheid was repealed, so **segregation** of facilities became illegal.
- The repeal of such apartheid measures which remained, such as the Population Registration Act and Group Areas Act, were facilitated by an Act of Parliament in June 1991.

Klerk had argued with colleagues that the end had to come quickly and as a whole rather than gradually or piecemeal. He felt a gradual reduction would lead to mistrust and delays. The speech of February 1990 could leave no one in doubt as to the scale of his intentions.

CODESA 1, 1991

The transition to democracy was hard and fraught with difficulties. December 1991 saw the creation of the Convention for a Democratic South Africa (CODESA) charged with preparing the ground for a new constitution. Inkhata, the PAC and the conservatives refused to attend: negotiations were bad-tempered among those who did.

Declaration of Intent

This was the biggest significant achievement of CODESA 1. It was a statement committing the government to reform. Although vaguely worded, it enabled de Klerk to seek a referendum to be held in March 1992 among white voters to see whether they supported the reform process: 69 per cent did so and gave him the mandate to continue.

Develop the detail

Below are a sample exam question and a paragraph written in answer to this question. The paragraph contains a limited amount of detail. Annotate the paragraph to add additional detail to the answer.

'The March 1992 referendum was the most important factor in the move towards full democracy in South Africa in the early 1990s.' How far do you agree with this statement?

The referendum held in March 1992 was important in the transition to democracy as 69 per cent of the voters agreed with the government's commitment to reform. However, there were other problems which needed to be addressed that the referendum didn't cover. There was still continuing violence. Neither Inkhata nor white conservative groups had joined CODESA 1. Talks themselves between the National Party and ANC were fraught. Lots of problems remained.

Support your judgement

Below are a sample exam question and three basic judgements. Read the exam question and the three judgements. Support the judgement that you agree with most strongly by adding a reason that justifies the judgement.

How accurate is it to say that by 1992 South Africa was close to civil war?

Overall, by 1992 South Africa was on the verge of civil war because

_____

_____

Although violence continued there was considerable hope for a peaceful settlement in South Africa by 1992 because

_____

_____

By 1992 some parts of South Africa were at war with each other and others not. For example, black South Africans in the townships were at war with each other because

_____

_____

Tip: Whichever option you choose you will have to weigh up both sides of the argument. You could use words such as 'whereas' or 'although' in order to help the process of evaluation.

Continued pressures on a new political settlement, 1992–94

The period 1992 to 1994 saw hard bargaining and many challenges, but the determination of both the National Party and ANC helped reach towards a settlement.

CODESA negotiations

The Declaration of Intent and success in the resulting referendum led to the creation of CODESA 2 in May 1992. It was charged with creating a working model for the new constitution. In the event it failed: Mandela accused the National Party of seeking to hold on to power while de Klerk was involved in battles within his own party to hold on to as much power as possible. However, even in the face of escalating violence, political leaders of the ANC and National Party knew this was the only hope for a peaceful settlement.

On 26 September, a Record of Understanding was issued, comprised of three principles:

1 Release of all political prisoners.
2 Physical restrictions of Zulu hostel dwellers who were held responsible for many of the Inkhata-inspired murders and attacks.
3 A banning of traditional weapons such as pangas which many people carried openly.

In return a future government was to guarantee employment and pension rights for existing public employees, and power sharing between the leading parties.

In February 1993 Mandela conceded that a future government would be one of 'National Unity' and would include members of all parties who received more than 5 per cent of the vote.

However, it was not easy to sell this agreement to members of the ANC or the National Party who continued to distrust each other, let alone the Conservative Party or Inkhata, both of which refused to have anything to do with it.

Nationalist divisions

De Klerk had difficulties persuading members of his own party to agree to a settlement. Many whites naturally feared for the future and many had already lost their livelihoods (see page 74):

- They were concerned for their safety in the event of an African black backlash.
- Many feared for their livelihoods as Africans became more skilled and could compete openly for jobs (see page 74).

- Many relied on the bureaucracy of apartheid or the security forces for employment. However, an agreement was reached here guaranteeing jobs and pensions.

The AWB meanwhile continued their terror campaign, while they were joined politically by the Conservatives led by General Constand Viljoen and Inkhata to form a Freedom Alliance. However, an incompetent military incursion into Bophuthatswana by the AWB to support the anti-settlement leader led to the Conservatives' withdrawal from the Freedom Alliance. The party split but most agreed to join in with the settlement process.

AWB incursion into Bophuthatswana

On 10 March 1994, 600 AWB members raided Bophuthatswana to rescue and reinstate the chief, Lucas Mongope. He had opposed the peace settlement and been arrested by the local forces who supported the ANC. The raid was unstructured: participants fired randomly at suspected ANC supporters before they themselves were routed by Bophuthatswana forces.

Continued violence

Violence continued throughout the period. While hundreds were being killed each month, three events in particular threatened to derail the settlement process:

- On 17 June 1992, Inkhata members killed 46 suspected ANC supporters in Boipatong. It was after this atrocity that Mandela suspended negotiations and supported mass protests which brought South Africa to a halt.
- On 7 September 1992, up to 100,000 ANC supporters marched to Bisho, the capital of Ciskei, whose leaders wished to maintain independence. Ciskei forces opened fire, killing 30 people.
- On 10 April 1993, the charismatic leader of MK, Chris Hani, was murdered by a white extremist.

However, those working for a settlement continued. Mandela was able to reassure his followers by emphasising that Hani's assassin was arrested following the evidence of a white witness, while de Klerk condemned white extremists. The result was a promise to hold elections the following April. There was therefore a deadline set for an agreement to be reached.

Establish a criteria

Below is a sample exam question which requires you to make a judgement. The key term in the question has been underlined. Defining the meaning of the key term can help you establish criteria that you can use to make a judgement.

Read the question, define the key term and then set out four criteria based on the key term, which you can use to reach and justify a judgement.

How accurate is it to say that there were <u>huge and continuing problems threatening</u> a peaceful settlement in South Africa in the years 1992 to 1994?

Definition:

Criteria to judge the extent to which huge and continuing problems threatening a peaceful settlement in South Africa in the years 1992 to 1994:

- _____
  _____

- _____
  _____

- _____
  _____

- _____
  _____

 Reach a judgement

Having defined the key term and established a series of criteria, you should now make a judgement on the question above.

Summarise your judgements below:

- Criteria 1:

- Criteria 2:

- Criteria 3:

- Criteria 4:

Finally, sum up your judgement. Based on the criteria, how accurate is it to say that there were huge and continuing problems threatening a peaceful settlement in South Africa in the years 1992 to 1994?

Tip: Remember you should weigh up evidence of continuing problems in your conclusion.

Constitutional agreement and elections

In September 1993 a Transitional Executive Council was set up to create the new political system in South Africa. Its principal goal was to ensure protection for minorities while accepting majority rule – in other words, the creation of a 'rainbow nation' in which everyone would be valued irrespective of race – again, the principles of the Freedom Charter of 1955.

The new constitution

- South Africa would be divided into nine provinces, each with its own elected government and civil service.
- A Bill of Rights would be protected by a Constitutional Court.
- The new system could only be amended by two-thirds majority of the popular vote.
- Guaranteed power sharing for five years: while the president would come from the leading party, the deputy president could come from any party with over 20 per cent of the vote and any party with more than 5 per cent could have a minister appointed.

Elections

Fully democratic elections were held on 26 April 1994. They were hugely anticipated. As expected, the ANC won fairly convincingly with 62.5 per cent of the vote; the National Party won 20.5 per cent so de Klerk became his deputy; Inkhata gained 10.5 per cent so Buthelezi became a government minister. The PAC, the party which had advocated continuing violence, won 1.25 per cent. The evidence seemed overwhelming that most people had voted for a peaceful and enduring settlement.

The Government of National Unity (GNU)

Nelson Mandela became president in a Government of National Unity. However, South Africa faced huge problems: 45 years of apartheid could not simply be effaced by a new constitution. Many Africans were frustrated by the slow pace of change: they lacked the education and skills to access most opportunities. Crime remained high. Many whites opted to leave. Newly appointed public servants were accused of corruption.

Creating unity

The transition to democracy was successful: there were no serious threats to the new system. Mandela's main task was to unify the country: one way was to galvanise countrywide support for the national rugby team which won the 1995 World Cup. A Truth and Reconciliation Commission was also set up in 1996 to investigate wrongdoing by all sides, not to exact retribution but to confront the past and move forward peacefully.

1999 elections

The ANC became the main political party in South Africa, maintaining its vision of multi-racialism. In the following elections of 1999, it gained enough seats to reform the constitution but chose not to do so. The National Party meanwhile collapsed with only 28 seats: the official opposition became the more liberal Democratic Party, itself with only 34. More importantly perhaps the parties of division such as the PAC and the Freedom Alliance received only 3 seats each.

International recognition

Representatives of 170 nations attended Nelson Mandela's inauguration as president. South Africa enjoyed widespread international support, not least through the good-will engendered by the personality of Mandela, who became a world elder statesman applauded everywhere. However, it was not just about Mandela. When he retired, his legacy was seamlessly continued. Countries recognised the achievement to move peacefully to democracy after so many years of conflict. The 'rainbow nation', it seemed, had become an example for the world.

Qualify your judgement (AO2)

Below is a sample exam question with the accompanying sources. Having read the question and the sources, complete the following activity:

How far could the historian make use of Sources 1 and 2 together to investigate the transition to democracy 1992 to 1994?

Below are two judgements about the value of Source 1 to a historian investigating the problems faced in transition to democracy, 1992 to 1994. Circle the judgement that best describes the value of the source, and explain why it is the best in the space provided.

1 Source 1 is valuable to a historian investigating the transition to democracy because it is written by a well-respected anti-apartheid activist who was an expert and was seeking an unbiased view.

2 Source 1 is partially valuable to a historian investigating the problems faced in the transition to democracy because it offers an even-handed account. It shows that the feared interracial violence did not materialise, but shows that other serious problems such as poor living conditions have not been addressed. However, it is also partial in its coverage, for example not discussing the often tortured political discussions.

The best judgement about the value of Source 1 is _____

because _____

_____

Now apply what you have learnt by writing a judgement about the value of Source 2 for a historian investigating the problems faced in the transition to democracy in the years 1992 to 1994.

SOURCE 1

From Archbishop Desmond Tutu, A Miracle Unfolding, *written in 1994. Tutu is an influential and well-respected anti-apartheid campaigner.*

The level of violence has been unacceptably high. Much of it is due to the machinations of a Third Force … mercifully none of the violence has been ethnic. [In Natal it had been Inkhata supporting Zulu pitted against ANC-supporting fellow Zulus.] It was not even by and large racial, except for that emanating from a lunatic fringes of the white right wing. A legitimate government, democratically elected, will be able to rehabilitate the police and army so that those organs of state can deal effectively with the violence because they have become more credible as neutral law enforcement and peacekeeping agencies. As it is, contrary to gloomy forecasts, the violence subsided quite considerably during the election (apart from the bombs planted by white right-wing elements). Indeed the violence in Natal dipped dramatically with the entry of the IFP [Inkhata] into the electoral process.

Apartheid has left us a horrendous legacy represented by massive homelessness, with seven million living in ghetto shacks, a huge educational crisis, unemployment, inadequate health care largely inaccessible to the most needy. The rural areas are poverty stricken, without running water, electricity or proper sewerage, so that cholera epidemics happen in a country that pioneered the heart transplant. It is quite bizarre.

SOURCE 2

From Daniel Reed, Beloved Country: South Africa's Silent Wars, *published in 1994. Daniel Reed is a journalist who was at the time working for the BBC.*

The last four years has seen the militarisation of South Africa's black townships increase to such an extent that the state security forces are now powerless to curb the influx of illegal weapons or the activities of local guerrilla units. Tactics have grown more sophisticated, the fighters more disciplined and hardened, the strategies more ruthless, including the 'ethnic cleansing' of civilians from occupied areas.

War has spawned a flourishing economy of gun-runners, professional looters, hired assassins, collectors of war levies and purveyors of battle-medicine, tapping a market worth many millions of Rand. South Africa is awash with cheap illegal firearms, from hand guns to assault rifles and grenade launchers. Violent crime has soared. Fighting has become a way of life, accompanied by a generalised war psychosis. In the East Rand townships [the main battle zone in the Transvaal] where two million people are caught up in a fierce territorial war, the average ten-year-old boy can strip down an AK-47 and put it back together again in less time than it takes to build a Lego house. Young children have become inured to the sound of gunfire and the smell of burning flesh.

Exam focus

Below is a sample A-level essay question followed by a model answer. Read the essay and the comments around it. Then tackle the task at the end.

How significant a threat to a peaceful settlement was violence from black and white groups in South Africa in the period 1990–94?

The continuing violence from both black and white groups who opposed a negotiated settlement posed a significant threat to the negotiations in the period 1990–94 and many indeed feared civil war. However, the determination of the leading politicians and the majority of South Africans to come to a peaceful agreement was stronger. Nevertheless the nature and impact of the violence must be considered in assessing its importance and whether or not the threat it posed was ever likely to derail the negotiations which were often in themselves fraught, with settlement seeming distant.

Shows understanding of the question.

Signposting essay development.

Significant groups from both the white and black African communities opposed a peaceful settlement. Many whites sought to continue the apartheid state, or alternatively be allocated their own white state within South Africa. Some of these groups such as the Conservatives opposed violence, but were nevertheless members of the Freedom Alliance which included groups such as the AWB who did not. They committed bombings and acts of intimidation. However, they failed dismally in an invasion of Bophuthatswana in March 1994 to support the anti-settlement leader: the incompetence of their attempt lost them credibility and considerable support. One result was that the Conservative Party joined the negotiating process and many whites formerly opposed to settlement changed their minds, however reluctantly. In this sense, although white fears were real, for example of a black backlash against them in a post-apartheid settlement, the threat they posed to any settlement was muted. Far more significant was that posed by black African opponents.

Explains nature of white violence.

Explains significance of white violence in terms of question.

Violence continued throughout the period. The military wing of the PAC for example targeted whites and black opponents. Much of the black-on-black violence however was perpetrated by ANC activists and members of the Inkhata Freedom Party (IFP) whom many felt were in a state of war. The IPF, formed in 1990, sought a Zulu homeland, but had ties with right-wing white groups including government officials who were accused of giving it covert support. While hundreds were being killed each month – 500 in August 1990 in the Rand alone – three events in particular threatened to derail the settlement process. On 17 June 1992, Inkhata members killed 46 suspected ANC supporters in Boipatong. It was after this atrocity that Mandela temporarily suspended negotiations and supported mass protests which brought South Africa to a halt. On 7 September 1992, 100,000 ANC supporters marched to Bisho, the capital of Ciskei, whose leaders wished to maintain independence. Ciskei forces opened fire, killing 30. On 10 April 1993 the leader of MK, Chris Hani, was murdered by a white extremist. However, those working for a settlement continued in their efforts. Mandela was able to reassure his followers by emphasising that Hani's assassin was arrested following the evidence of a white witness, while de Klerk condemned white extremists. The result was a promise to hold elections the following April. There was therefore a deadline set for an agreement to be reached

Shows extent of violence.

In this sense the significance of the threat caused by violence appeared to be averted. However, there were other threats, not least the acrimony between the two main parties, the ANC and National Party. It was clear that mutual trust would be tenuous and both were trying to reconcile hardliners within their own groups. Many ANC supporters

Strikes a balance by showing other significant threats.

wanted a settlement which would reward their struggles. They looked for example to the huge inequalities of wealth and inequalities in living standards and sought immediate improvements. White conservatives looked to maintain minority rule if not to safeguard their own position and safety.

It was the determination of the leading parties to reach a settlement to which as many groups as possible could agree which ultimately defused the violence. On 26 September 1992, a Record of Understanding was issued comprised of three principles: release of all political prisoners; physical restrictions of Zulu hostel dwellers who were held responsible for many of the Inkhata-inspired murders and attacks; and a banning of traditional weapons such as pangas which many people carried openly. A future government meanwhile was to guarantee employment and pension rights for existing public employees, and power sharing between the leading parties. This satisfied many whites who had feared for their livelihoods and safety; some in the National Party even hoped for an electoral victory.

> This paragraph drifts a little – could be related more closely to the question.

In February 1993 Mandela conceded that a future government would be one of 'National Unity' and would include members of all parties who received more than 5 per cent of the vote. This was significant in the reduction in violence in that the IFP and PAC agreed to join the reform process and fight elections. It was the new constitution with its emphasis on power sharing which brought formerly hostile groups into the negotiating process and therefore reduced violence. In the 1994 elections, for example, Inkhata received 10 per cent of the vote and Chief Buthelezi became a government minister. De Klerk meanwhile became deputy president as the leader of the second largest party, the National Party.

> Explains how the settlement reduced levels of violence.

During the period 1990 to 1994 many feared South Africa was in the grip of civil war. The continued violence seemed out of control and a real threat to the settlement process. However, negotiations continued through the various forms of CODESA and regular meetings until a settlement could be achieved to which all involved could subscribe. It was this settlement with the promised power sharing and representation in government according to support which brought most of the formerly violent groups into the peace process. Therefore while the violence may have posed a significant threat, the determination of those committed to peace was stronger, and the new constitutional arrangements came into force in April 1994 after the first free and fully democratic elections.

> Fully propelled conclusion with valid supported judgement.

This is a focused, well-written essay which addresses all the issues although one paragraph does drift slightly into narrative. It explains the significance of the threat occasioned by violence well, and looks for a balance by considering other threats. Its judgement is valid on the basis of what has been argued. This essay would attain Level 5.

Exam focus (A01 & A03)

It is not only important to develop an accurate written style but also useful to practise how to structure an answer. Identify the pattern in this answer by counting the sentences in each paragraph. It is also important to include some supporting information. Look at paragraphs two, three and four and highlight the supporting information that is used to develop each explanation.

Glossary

Allies The USA, Britain, the USSR and other countries who supported them during the Second World War.

Betterment Term to describe government-led improvements in agriculture and living conditions in the tribal homelands.

Black Consciousness Movement based on Black Power in the USA in which African people took increasing pride in their culture and identity. This was particularly associated with Steve Biko and the South African Students' Association (SASO).

Black Sash An anti-apartheid group made up of white female activists.

Blackspots Areas outside the land officially designated for settlement by Africans, where they nevertheless had managed to acquire land: these were abolished by the 1950 Group Areas Act.

Boer War War 1899–1902 between Great Britain and Boer Settlers over independence for South Africa.

Broederbund Highly influential and secretive Afrikaner organisation.

Cato Manor Area near Durban, the scene of riots against the closure of beer halls in 1959.

Commonwealth Association of members and former members of the British Empire.

Communism A political philosophy that endorses a state-controlled economy and rewards people according to their perceived value.

Covenant Solemn oath, in this sense the agreement made between God and Boers in 1838.

Decolonisation Former colonies winning their independence.

Dominion Largely self-governing country within the British Empire, recognising the monarch as head of state.

Dutch Reformed Church The Church supported by many Afrikaners which justified apartheid.

Eiselen Report The report which suggested that education should ideally be taught in the homelands, be taught in tribal languages and reflect the needs of Africans.

Great Trek The 1830s migration of Boer famers into the heartland of South Africa, away from British rule.

Guerrilla warfare Fighting using techniques such as ambush and bombings, avoiding direct large-scale conflict.

Hinterland An area inside the country, away from coastal areas.

Inkhata Zulu nationalist organisation which developed into the Inkhata Freedom Party in 1990: it opposed the ANC in the 1980s and sought an independent Zulu homeland.

Intaba movement Resistance movement in East Pondoland: Intaba is an African word for 'mountain'.

Integrationalist The belief that the different races should work and co-operate together.

'Laager mentality' Referring to the increasing readiness of Afrikaners to defend their regime and beliefs; 'laager' refers to a defensive encampment.

Mission schools Schools run by various churches to educate black African children.

Necklaced Vigilante punishment by setting victims on fire by enveloping them in petrol-soaked tyres.

Oil crisis The economic crisis of 1973 caused by rocketing worldwide prices for oil.

Pass An internal passport for black Africans in South Africa – in 1952 it was extended to women.

Pastoral environment Rural life based on small-scale farming.

Security Council The executive power of the UN dominated by the USA, Russia, Britain, France and China, each of which has a veto to override decisions.

Shebeens Illegal drinking dens, often targeted by anti-apartheid protesters as places where black African men were persuaded to over-spend their money at the expense of supporting their families.

Total Onslaught The fear that there was a total co-ordinated attack orchestrated by communists to destroy apartheid.

Total Strategy The all-embracing government response to the Total Onslaught, fighting it within South Africa and abroad by all possible means at the state's disposal.

Township Area where black Africans lived separately from other races.

Tribal reserves Areas designated the original homelands of those making up South Africa's African population.

UN General Council The parliament of the United Nations in which all member countries vote.

United Democratic Front (UDF) Organisation created in 1983 within South Africa to co-ordinate the struggle against apartheid.

United Nations International organisation set up in 1945 to promote world peace and co-operation between nations.

Voortrekker monument Huge monument built in Pretoria in 1938 to celebrate the Great Trek and Battle of Blood River.

Key figures

Steve Biko (1946–77) Biko was a medical student who was a fierce opponent of apartheid. An Africanist, he formed the South African Students' Organisation in 1968 solely for African students. Biko died in police custody in August 1977. He became a martyr for the anti-apartheid movement.

P.W. Botha (1916–2006) P.W. Botha was a National Party politician. As defence minister from 1966 he built up a strong relationship with the security forces. He became prime minster in 1978 and president in 1984. Botha's time in office was characterised by limited reform, robust repression at home and an extension of activity abroad to secure South Africa's borders and fight anti-apartheid organisations. He retired after suffering a stroke in 1989.

Chief Buthelezi (1928–) Buthelezi was a Zulu tribal leader and politician who served as Chief Executive of the homeland of KwaZulu from 1970. In 1990 Buthelezi formed the Inkhata Freedom Party which was accused of much of the violence resulting from conflict with the ANC. In 1994 Buthelezi became Minister of Home Affairs in Mandela's government.

F.W. de Klerk (1936–) De Klerk rose unspectacularly through the ranks of the National Party before becoming executive president in August 1989. He followed the New Course, abolishing apartheid and seeking dialogue to usher in a new democratic South Africa. His efforts resulted in the 1994 agreement. In 1993 de Klerk and Nelson Mandela jointly received the Nobel Peace Prize. After April 1994 he became Mandela's deputy president. He retired from all public offices in 1997.

Chief Albert Luthuli (1898–1967) Luthuli was a teacher who became president of the ANC in 1952. However, his effectiveness during his period of office was reduced by his constant house arrest at his home at Groutville. Luthuli was awarded the Nobel Peace Prize in 1961, but was increasingly an isolated figure as other ANC leaders were imprisoned and the organisation itself went into exile. Luthuli died in mysterious circumstances in 1967.

D.F. Malan (1874–1959) Malan was the National Party leader who won the 1948 election and introduced the apartheid state. He had opposed South Africa's entry into the Second World War and supported Afrikaner culture and identity. Malan presided over the introduction of key apartheid legislation before retiring in 1954.

Nelson Mandela (1918–2013) Mandela was a leading figure in the ANC. He helped form the ANC Youth League (ANCYL) in 1943 which advocated direct action and in 1960 the ANC military wing, the MK. Mandela was arrested in 1962. He was sentenced to life imprisonment on Robben Island before emerging in 1990 as the leading ANC negotiator for a democratic South Africa. He became the first president of the democratic South Africa and is widely credited with uniting the country.

Joe Slovo (1926–95) Slovo held office in the trade union movement before enlisting in the Second World War. He joined the Communist Party in 1942 and began to work closely with the ANC. In 1986 Slovo became Secretary-General of the SACP, and in 1987 Chief of Staff of MK. In the first post-apartheid government he became Minister of Housing.

Robert Sobukwe (1924–78) Sobukwe was a university teacher who joined the ANC, but developed strong Africanist policies and in 1958 helped form the PAC, whose president he became in 1959. After the PAC was banned, Sobukwe was arrested and imprisoned. He was eventually released under house arrest in 1969: he was refused permission to travel abroad even when offered lecturing positions in US universities.

Oliver Tambo (1917–93) Tambo was an activist who helped form the ANC Youth League in 1943. In 1955 he became ANC Secretary-General and in 1958 Deputy President. He was sent abroad to develop overseas support for the ANC. He led the organisation in exile until returning to South Africa in 1990. He had become president in 1967 on the death of Chief Luthuli.

Archbishop Desmond Tutu (1931–) Desmond Tutu was a senior Anglican churchman. He was a vociferous opponent of apartheid but always advocated reconciliation and opposed violence. He won the Nobel Peace Prize in 1984. After the formation of a democratic South Africa, Tutu headed the Truth and Reconciliation Commission.

Hendrik Verwoerd (1901–66) Verwoerd was both the principal theoretician and architect of apartheid. In 1950 he became Minister for Bantu Affairs, being responsible for much of the apartheid legislation. In 1958 he became prime minister. His government left the Commonwealth and initiated a republic. Verwoerd survived one assassination attempt in 1961 but died after another in September 1966.

John Vorster (1915–83) Vorster was appointed Minister of Justice in 1961 and Minister of Police and Prisons in 1966. He became prime minister on the assassination of Hendrik Verwoerd in September 1966. Vorster presided over what was probably the most secure period of apartheid in the 1960s and early 1970s.

Timeline

1899–1902	Boer War
1910	Creation of the Dominion of South Africa
1912	Creation of the ANC
1913	Native Land Act
1923	Natives (Urban Areas) Act
1936	Natives Trust and Land Act
1944	ANC Youth League (ANCYL) formed
1948	National Party electoral victory
1949	Prohibition of Mixed Marriages Act
1950	Population Registration Act
	Immorality Act
	Suppression of Communism Act
1951	Bantu Authorities Act
	Defiance campaign
1952	National Laws Amendment Act (also known as Abolition of Passes and Co-ordination of Documents Act)
1953	Bantu Education Act
1955	Freedom Charter adopted
1956	Tomlinson Committee report on Bantustans
1956	Women's pass protests
1957	Zeerust uprising
1959	Formation of PAC
	Promotion of Self-Government Act
1960	'Winds of change' speech
	Sharpeville massacre
	State of emergency, banning of ANC and PAC
1961	Suppression of the East Pondoland rebellion
	Ending of the Treason Trial
	South Africa left the Commonwealth and became a republic
	Formation of MK
1962	Poqo attack on white settlement of Paarl
	Arrest of Nelson Mandela
1963	Transkei made 'independent' Bantustan
	Rivonia Trial and imprisonment of Mandela and other ANC leaders
	Formation of Organisation of African Unity (OAU)
	UN resolution 1761 calling for voluntary sanctions on South Africa
1967	ANC alliance with ZAPU
1969	Morogoro Conference
	Formation of SASO
1974	Independence from Portugal of Angola and Zimbabwe

1976	Soweto uprising
1977	Death of Steve Biko in police custody
	Transkei given full independence
	UN Resolution 177 arms embargo on South Africa
	Gleneagles Agreement on severing Commonwealth sporting links with South Africa
	Announcement of Total Onslaught and Total Strategy to combat it
1978	Visit of ANC leadership to Vietnam leading to an intensification of their struggle against apartheid
	Kassinga massacre in Namibia
	UN Resolution 435 calling for a peace settlement in Namibia
	'Muldergate' scandal undermined government of John Vorster
1979	Rhodesian settlement with formation of Zimbabwe
	Venda given full independence
1981	Ciskei given full independence
1984	New constitution with P.W. Botha becoming executive president
1986	US Congress overrode President Reagan's veto on sanctions
	Abolition of pass laws
	Severe financial crisis caused by US banks' refusal to renew loans
	Announcement of state of emergency
1988	Nelson Mandela 70th birthday concert at Wembley Arena
1989	F.W. de Klerk became president committed to change
1990	De Klerk's 'New Course' announced in inaugural speech as president: release of Nelson Mandela
1991	CODESA 1
1992	Referendum among white voters accepted the need for change
	Creation of CODESA 2
1993	Creation of Transitional Executive Council to prepare for democracy in South Africa
	Murder of Chris Hani, MK leader
1994	First elections under new non-racial constitution: creation of Government of National Unity with Nelson Mandela as president

Paper 2 mark scheme

Paper 2 requires two mark schemes, one for the AO2 assessments in Section A and another for Section B's AO1 assessment.

AO1 mark scheme

REVISED

- **Analytical focus** (which means engaging with the key features or topics of the question and addressing the concept in the question specifically).
- **Accurate detail** (which means using supporting detailed knowledge to explain and develop your argument).
- **Supported judgement** (which means making judgements through the essay about each key point or factor, as well as at the end of the essay).
- Argument and structure (which means an essay which is organised, logical and covers the necessary points in a controlled manner).

Level	Marks	Description
1	1–3	• Simplistic statements. • Very limited accurate and relevant knowledge. • There is either no overall judgement, or it is very basic. • Very little structure or argument.
2	4–7	• Descriptive statements about key features. • Mostly accurate and relevant knowledge, but limited in terms of range and depth. • An overall judgement is presented, but with limited support. The judgement lacks clear criteria. • The work shows the beginnings of structure and a limited attempt to create an argument.
3	8–12	• Some analysis of key features. • Mostly accurate and relevant knowledge is used in a way that shows some understanding of the question. The range and depth may be limited in places. • An overall judgement is presented. It is supported with an attempt to establish criteria. • Some structure and a generally clear argument.
4	13–16	• Analysis of key features. • Sufficient accurate and relevant knowledge is used to answer most aspects of the question. • An overall judgement is presented. It is based on valid criteria, but may only be partially supported. • A well-structured essay with a clear argument, although in places the argument may lack precision.
5	17–20	• Sustained analysis of key features. • Sufficient accurate and relevant knowledge is used to answer all key aspects of the question. • An overall judgement is presented. It is based on valid criteria, and is fully supported. The relative significance of the criteria may be considered whilst reaching the judgement. • A well-structured essay with a clear argument which is communicated with precision.

AO2 mark scheme

- **Analytical focus** (which means identifying and explaining the key features of the source, handling it as an interpretation rather than just a source of information).
- **Accurate detail** (which means using your own knowledge to explain the features of the source and to evaluate them).
- **Supported judgement** (which means evaluating the value of the source through the essay and also at the end).

Level	Marks	Description
1	1–3	• Surface level comprehension of the sources, demonstrated by quoting or paraphrasing, without analysis. • Some relevant knowledge of the historical context is included, but links to the sources are limited. • There is either no overall evaluation of the sources or discussion of reliability and utility is very basic.
2	4–7	• Some understanding of the sources, demonstrated by selecting and summarising relevant information. • Some relevant knowledge of the historical context is linked to the sources to support or challenge the detail they include. • An overall judgement is presented, but with limited support. Discussion of reliability and utility are based on a limited discussion of provenance and may reflect invalid assumptions.
3	8–12	• Understanding of the sources, demonstrated by some analysis of key points, explaining their meaning and valid inferences. • Relevant knowledge of the historical context is used to support inferences. Contextual knowledge is also used to expand on support or challenge matters of detail. • An overall judgement is presented, which relates to the nature and purpose of the sources. The judgement is based on valid criteria, but the support is likely to be limited.
4	13–16	• Analysis of the sources, demonstrated by examining their evidence to make reasoned inferences. Valid distinctions are made between information and opinion. Treatment of the two sources may be uneven. • Relevant knowledge of the historical context is used to reveal and discuss the limitations of sources' content. The answer attempts to interpret the source material in the context of the values and assumptions of the society it comes from. • An overall judgement regarding the interpretation is presented which is supported by valid criteria. Evaluation of the sources reflects how much weight the evidence of the sources can bear. Aspects of the judgement may have limited support.
5	17–20	• Confident interrogation of both sources demonstrated by reasoned inferences. The answer shows a range of ways the sources can be used, making valid distinctions between information and opinion. • Relevant knowledge of the historical context is used to reveal and discuss the limitations of sources' content. The answer interprets the source material in the context of the values and assumptions of the society it comes from. • An overall judgement regarding the interpretation is presented which is supported by valid criteria. Evaluation of the sources reflects how much weigh the evidence of the sources can bear and may distinguish between the degrees to which aspects of the sources can be useful.

Answers

Page 7, Spot the mistake

This response does not address the question. It simply relates the types of different racial groups and asserts they faced discrimination.

Page 9, Spot the inference

Points 1 and 5 can be inferred; the source implies English South Africans embraced industry and commerce earlier although more Afrikaners are now successfully following their lead. The second point is a summary of the source while the third is a paraphrase. The fourth point cannot be justified from the source.

Page 13, Explain the difference

Source 1 is written in legal language and doesn't consider the human effects of its terms. Source 2 is from an impassioned critic who considers the human impact of apartheid laws over time – in this case on children in the same family and those unable to marry.

Page 15, Identify an argument

The first answer is really assertion because it makes a statement but doesn't direct the ensuing content at it. The second makes the argument, supported by evidence, that self-governance and independence was not a primary goal of the creation of the homelands.

Page 17, Eliminate irrelevance

It would be very accurate to say that the government passed wide-ranging acts of suppression during the 1950s. The intention was to outlaw anti-apartheid movements. They did this primarily through the Suppression of Communism Act 1950. The regime hoped to equate anti-apartheid activity with communism, which was seen as a threat to the West during the Cold War. ~~The Cold War meant war without fighting, in which the USSR and West were using international issues to engender one-upmanship on each other such as the Berlin Blockade and Airlift of 1948–49. By being tough on communism, South Africa hoped to prove itself a reliable ally with the West.~~ However, the Act defined communism as any threat to political, economic or social order – in other words a very wide definition. Other measures reinforced suppression – such as the Censorship Acts in 1955 and 1956 to prevent critical material being imported into South Africa and the Riotous Assemblies Act to prevent any meetings which it was felt might engender hostility between the races, and preventing any 'banned' persons from addressing public meetings.

Page 21, You're the examiner

This paragraph suggests a Level 5 response. The sources are interrogated in terms of the question, and a judgement is reached concerning limitations in Source 1 in relation to the focus of the investigation. It is well-organised, with some context – for example, the ANC being multi-racial, as opposed to the PAC which was only open to black Africans.

Page 29, RAG – rate the timeline

1959 April Creation of PAC

1960 March Sharpeville massacre

1960 April State of emergency declared

1960 April ANC and PAC declared illegal organisations

1960 South Africa left the Commonwealth

1961 January Pondoland rebellion suppressed

1961 July John Vorster appointed Minister of Justice

1962 June Sabotage Act

1963 May General Laws Amendment Act

1965 January Bantu Laws Amendment Act

Page 31, Explain the difference

Macmillan was a foreign prime minister talking about international changes he was aware of and their implications for South Africa as he understood them. Verwoerd was committed to the apartheid state and dismissed Macmillan's concerns. His government was fully committed to the continuation of apartheid. It may also be defensive in that it acknowledges white Africans have nowhere else to go.

Page 33, Eliminate irrelevance

The ANC leadership was increasingly frustrated by government repression which defeated peaceful protest. The government had passed a raft of measures in the early 1960s which banned protest and had outlawed groups such as the ANC. The security forces had always been prepared to use violence, as for example in the massacre at Sharpeville, and activists were becoming increasingly militant and frustrated with peaceful tactics. At Sharpeville the authorities fired on peaceful protesters, killing 69 – ~~although the authorities said the demonstrators were armed and threatening.~~ Indeed, violence was already widespread in many rural areas, for example in Eastern Pondoland where the rebellion led by the Intaba movement had been defeated by superior government forces. The decision to begin an armed struggle was to some degree a case of leaders catching up with the demands of their supporters. There were, however, other factors such as the failure of peaceful protest. The government sometimes arrested leaders after they had agreed to meet with them. Accordingly MK began their campaign on 16 December 1961. ~~Bombings took place in government buildings in Durban and Port Elizabeth, including an electricity sub-station. In the next 18 months 200 attacks took place.~~

Page 35, Identify an argument

The first response contains an argument – that the authorities wished to stop violent protest by recourse to the law and this was more important to them than international condemnation. The second answer is mainly description.

Page 37, Write the question

Answers should focus on the effectiveness of the PAC in exile or on the types of activities they were undertaking; you could also use the sources to discuss how the sources could be used to show how prepared they were to combat the South African government during this period.

Page 39, Flaw in the argument

This answer is weakened because of the assertion that the economy was fragile because it relied on foreign investment: the candidate has conversely explained how this investment had made South Africa wealthy. It would need a balanced argument to show why this reliance was dangerous.

Page 39, You're the examiner

This response is well-organised and addresses with confidence the demands of the question. It has a good range and communication is clear and precise. This response is suggestive of Level 5.

Page 41, Spot the inference

The first and fifth statements can be inferred. The third is paraphrasing the source, the fourth is a summary, while the second cannot be justified from the source.

Page 45, Explain the difference

The Broederbund source is a policy document to justify the teaching in Afrikaans and implies in part the aim was to keep black Africans in subservience. However, the second source is from a teacher explaining the impossibilities of this.

Page 53, Flaw in the argument

The question is about challenges to the National Party in the 1970s. The argument is flawed because it doesn't say how significant the polarisation in white politics was becoming during the 1970s. For example, the official opposition in 1977 had 17 seats: the National Party had 134. When the response goes on to widening the power base it states that the purpose of this was to isolate black Africans even more. This is not the question focus.

Page 57, Write the question

The question should be about South Africa's role in Namibia or Southern Africa generally. For example, how useful they are in showing the contradictions in South Africa's policy or to explain the distrust South Africa generated amongst its neighbours. The sources would be too narrow to consider South Africa's foreign relations outside Southern Africa.

Page 69, Write the question

Your question should reflect the reasons why President Botha wished to reform apartheid and how Mandela responded to the offer of freedom. Clearly he did not feel the reforms went far enough. The questions could relate to how the historian could use the sources to investigate the extent or support for Botha's reforms.

Page 71, You're the examiner

This is a confident conclusion which shows the interconnectedness of causes. It brings together information which was presumably discussed earlier. It is well-focused and would probably attain Level 5.